My Journey
in Grace

It is good for our hearts to be strengthened by grace.
(Hebrews 13:9)

Terrell D. Suggs

Founders Press

Committed to historic Baptist principles
Cape Coral, Florida

Published by

Founders Press
Committed to historic Baptist principles

P.O. Box 150931 • Cape Coral, FL 33915
Phone (239) 772-1400 • Fax: (239) 772-1140
Electronic Mail: founders@founders.org or
Website: http://www.founders.org
©2008 Founders Press

Printed in the United States of America

10 ISBN: 0-9785711-0-X
13 ISBN: 978-0-9785711-0-8

Introduction

My Journey in Grace is essentially an account of my theological pilgrimage as a Christian and Southern Baptist. Southern Baptists are the people I know and love. God in His good providence allowed me to be born and reared a Southern Baptist. It was my privilege to attend a Southern Baptist college and seminary. My ministry in Southern Baptist churches has spanned more than forty years. I love my denomination and owe a great deal to it.

As a denomination, we enjoy a remarkable and unique heritage. In my study, it has been my delight to discover our Southern Baptist Convention founding fathers and examine their lives and theology. Much of what these godly men believed has been dismissed or forgotten today. I believe their theology was biblically impeccable. For Southern Baptists to hear their historic voices again is my prayer. Primarily I have focused on what is termed the "doctrines of grace." Others call it "sovereign grace" or the "Reformed Faith." Still others refer to it as "Calvinism," a term that has regretfully been greatly misunderstood. But when properly understood in its historical context, it defines the faith of early Southern Baptists.

This includes doctrines such as the sovereignty of God, foreknowledge, total depravity, unconditional election, particular redemption, effectual calling and perseverance of the saints. This theology can be summed up in what Jonah discovered in the belly of the great fish thousands of years ago, that "Salvation is of the Lord" (Jonah 2:9), or in Paul's statement in Ephesians 2:8, "For it is by grace you have been saved."

Many evangelical Christians of our day are praying for revival. The passionate prayer of the prophet is mine as well:

> Oh, that you would rend the heavens and come down, that the mountains would tremble before you! As when fire sets twigs ablaze and causes water to boil, come down to make your name known to your enemies and cause the nations to quake before you" (Isaiah 64:1–2).

Many of us believe, however, there will never be a lasting revival until we have a doctrinal reformation. Without a solid foundation no structure is built well. Until our people are again doctrinally grounded, especially in the doctrines of grace, we will never fully realize the truth that sets us free (John 8:32).

A growing number of contemporary Southern Baptists share my views and concerns. It is thrilling to testify that God is bringing doctrinal reformation. However, many more voices need to be heard. That is why I feel compelled to share *My Journey in Grace*. May the Lord use this testimony, along with other works, to again show how amazing His grace truly is.

As you can see, this is by no means an exhaustive work. I do not claim to have any unique credentials. My goal is simply to tell my story and be helpful to others in pointing to the truth of God's Word. I have been a pastor and am now a director of missions, speaking from the grass roots level of Southern Baptist life echoing the same cry of Hosea, "My people are destroyed from lack of knowledge" (Hosea 4:6).

I identify with the Psalmist when he said, "I believe, therefore I said" (Psalm 116:10). The Lord uses the uniqueness of each of His children. As Andrew was a pilot-light to the great apostle Peter, perhaps the Lord will be pleased, in His providence, to use this work to cause some to embrace the doctrines of grace and, in turn, be used to light gospel fires across our world. It is with this assurance that I write.

You will note in the pages that follow that I have quoted extensively from many great books. I am grateful to the publishers who have allowed me to quote at length and share a portion of what has been enormoursly helpful to me in in my journey. These books are worth more to me than pots of diamonds and mounds of gold. If I could convince you to find and purchase and read carefully even a few of them, my time working on this book will be well-spent. Throughout Christian history our Lord has been pleased to raise up many men of incredible intellect and amazing spiritual insight who have left their works for us in print. It would be almost impossible to name them all. From their pens we have vast resources. To neglect these priceless works is to deprive ourselves of rich spiritual treasure. We must drink continually from their thirst quenching waters and be edified by their soul satisfying nourishment.

May the Lord give you, the reader, a Berean spirit (Acts 17:11) as you examine these historic, as well as biblical, truths. Please do not examine Calvinism as the three blind men examined an elephant. They had never heard of an elephant but were taken to a zoo and asked to tell what they thought one was. The first man felt of the elephant's tail and concluded that he was a rope. The next felt of his leg and thought he was a tree. The third man felt the trunk of the elephant and declared that he was a fire hose. None of them were right but they all thought they were. Their obvious mistake was a lack of thoroughness. Many have examined Calvinism in a similar way. However, the honest student of the Word is compelled to look at the total picture. Please do not claim an adequate knowledge of the entire Calvinistic system by a mere knowledge of the caricatures or stereotypes. Too often it has been wrongfully condemned by those who only had a partial or skewed knowledge. It takes a great deal of prayerful and intense study to gain a proper understanding.

As I write, it is my hope and prayer that this book will serve to spark interest and motivate some to delve deeper into Scripture, Baptist history and into some of the great theological classics. I am deeply honored to have you travel with me on my journey. That it will be enlightening and enriching to you is my sincere prayer. As I begin *My Journey in Grace* I am reminded of the Psalmist's invitation: "Come and listen, all you who fear God; let me tell you what he has done for me" (Psalm 66:16). Many years ago, as a child, God started me on an incredible journey in grace that He lovingly planned in eternity. It has been the delight of my life. With all my heart I want to share what I have discovered.

Contents

Part One

A Personal Journey

I

My Discovery of the Doctrines of Grace

When the Lord called me to preach as a teenager, I wanted to be the best I could be. My sense of calling and need to preach has remained at a high level. I love preaching and preachers. Through the years there have been scores of preachers for whom I have had unusual admiration. They have been models and mentors for me. While I have always tried to maintain my own uniqueness, other men's beliefs and practices have greatly intrigued and inspired me.

I have, at times, very naively and almost unquestionably followed them. I would go to their churches, devour their books and study their theology and methods. At times, I must confess I did not glean truths for myself from the Scriptures. To my deep regret, what I believed, preached and practiced was not always thoroughly grounded in the Bible itself but on what some successful preacher was espousing. It was especially this way in the area of theology.

My theological education in college and seminary left something to be desired. However, in those early years I did adopt the expository method as my primary way of preaching. In this way, I had to study every verse. Often texts that dealt with such subjects as the sovereignty of God or His foreknowledge puzzled me. This was especially so in the light of all the man-centered "free-willism" I had been taught. I found that commentators would often evade these subjects. Of all the sermons I had read or heard, very few dealt with them. It became obvious that terms such as "predestination" or "election" are very scary subjects to many people.

Responses of impatience and even anger would sometimes result when I preached on or discussed these subjects. I have been accused of being foolish and even a cultist for believing them. In my study, however, I saw that the biblical writers never hesitated to talk very freely, openly and often about them, even to new believers (1 Thessalonians 1; Ephesians 1, 1 Peter 1, etc.). If they are so much a part of the Bible, I reasoned, why don't we freely talk about them?

In my study, I had mixed emotions. Sometimes I found myself struggling, even to the point of tears. I remember waves of terror sweeping over me as I pondered the reality of hell and eternal judgment. In wrestling with the subject of the fairness of God I would agonize over such questions as: "Why evil?" "Why the devil?" "Why suffering?" "Why sin?" "Why the fall of man in the garden?" "Why did God elect some and not all?" At other times, I would become overwhelmed with joy.

More and more I was amazed at the wonder of God's free grace to undeserving sinners. I wanted to delve into the deep things of God and find answers. I knew I could never completely understand, but I wanted to try. My sincere prayer was for God to unveil His Word to me. The more I searched and prayed, the more I discovered books and commentaries that powerfully spoke to me. Some had been on my bookshelves for years, though I had never read them.

The Lord began to use the writings of such men as C. H. Spurgeon and A. W. Pink to fill me with truth. The Scriptures began to open as never before. I was thrilled beyond words. God became more real to me than ever and the gospel of His sovereign grace virtually jumped off the pages with clarity and power. I began to see the person of Jesus Christ unveiled in all His mighty splendor. I saw in Scripture that Christ is not the weak "Savior" that we often hear about; the One standing on the wayside of life trying to save the world but "sovereign sinners" won't "let" Him.

Rather, I saw the Christ of the Bible as the Savior of His people, the Church (Matthew 1:21; Ephesians 5:25). In the Covenant of Grace, He came to save those whom the Father had given Him. He will most certainly accomplish this (John 6:37; 17:1–20). He will not be defeated. His kingdom is forever. Not only will He reign someday, but He reigns now (Acts 2:32–35). He is the Christ who has been exalted to the highest place and given a name that is above every name (Philippians 2:9).

I began to understand the reality that God is sovereign. I was especially challenged by A. W. Pink's book *The Sovereignty of God*. Never had I read such a work. What was so powerful and compelling was his overwhelming scriptural proof of every claim he made. I had never seen these things before. I could not deny them. How had I missed seeing all this in my study of Scripture? Where had all these great books and writers been all my life?

At first I wondered about the direction in which I was headed. I felt alone in my beliefs. Were there other Southern Baptists that shared my views? The more I searched, the more I began discovering other people of like faith. They were not in abundance but they were there. I thank my God always for each one.

A pastor friend introduced me to the outstanding writings of J. P. Boyce and J. L. Dagg. Boyce was the founder of The Southern Baptist Theological Seminary in Louisville, Kentucky and Dagg was the first writing Southern Baptist theologian. Both of these men were among the great early leaders of our convention. The more I studied Baptist history and the theology of our founders, the more I saw that I believed what they believed. I am forever indebted to these men who have given us some of the finest theological works in all of Christian history.

In 1983, I received information about the Southern Baptist Founders Conference. I was elated. I will never forget my first time to attend the conference. It was held at Rhodes College in Memphis, Tennessee. I was thrilled to attend. Here was a conference filled with Southern Baptists that believed just as I did and shared my concerns. They were committed to doctrinal reformation in our Southern Baptist life. Sermons were preached, papers read, testimonies given, and books made available on the biblically sound faith of our founding fathers. I couldn't believe my ears. I am edified each time I attend this wonderful conference that continues to meet regionally.

Indeed I came to see that the doctrines of grace were not incidental in the lives of Baptists from the seventeenth to the twentieth centuries. The rafters of Southern Baptist churches once rang with these great truths. Seminary and college professors were meticulous in teaching young preachers to articulate the gospel of sovereign grace. This was the gospel that Baptists carried to the ends of the earth. These doctrines were the very foundation of everything in Baptist life. Oh, that it would be so again!

How thrilling it was to make these exciting discoveries. The more I studied, reflected, prayed and talked with others, the more I became convinced that God was showing me truths that had long been neglected. The vast majority of Southern Baptists and much of the Christian world knew little, if anything, about the doctrines of grace. The Lord began to make it quite obvious to me that He did not want me to hide these truths "under a bushel," but to hold them high for all to see. This has been and continues to be my desire as God, by His grace, gives me opportunity to serve Him in the spread of gospel for His glory.

Part Two

A Historical Journey

2

The Doctrines of Grace
In Southern Baptist History

History is a subject that is unappreciated by many. Because of this, we tend not to heed what it teaches. However, it is of immeasurable importance. One of the most valuable aspects of history is the perspective it gives since we cannot know where we are going unless we know where we have been. This is no less true as we study the history of those who shaped our beloved Southern Baptist Convention.

Baptist history is rooted in the Protestant Reformation, which, many believe, was the greatest spiritual awakening in the history of the church. The word *alone* (*sola* in Latin) provides a key to understanding the main themes of Reformation doctrine: Scripture alone (*sola Scriptura*), grace alone (*sola gratia*), faith alone (*sola fide*), Christ alone (*solus Christus*) and to the glory of God alone (*soli Deo gloria*). These great truths form the heart of Calvinism.

Our Historical Roots in Calvinism

When our Convention was organized in 1845, the doctrines of grace saturated the hearts and minds of Southern Baptists. There are scores of historical sources that prove this. A Sunday School Board workers manual written as late as 1918 states that "nearly all Baptists believe what are usually termed the 'doctrines of grace'."[1]

---

[1] *The New Convention Normal Manual for Sunday School Workers* (Nashville, TN: Sunday School Board, Southern Baptist Convention, 1918), 307.

Dr. James Leo Garrett, in an address in 1982 at Southwestern Baptist Theological Seminary named five major movements rising on the SBC scene. These were the Charismatic Movement, the Dispensational Movement, the Biblical Inerrancy Movement, the Keswick Movement, and the Calvinistic Movement. In referring to the Calvinistic Movement he said:

> Now, this is a movement that asserts the truth and the viability of the strong Calvinism that we can find in our Southern Baptist past and our English Baptist past. It is in a sense an effort to recapture the Calvinism that has been lost in the last three quarters of the century, or so, and to cover this involves a new emphasis on the writings of John L. Dagg and James P. Boyce and of the 1644 and 1689 Particular Baptist confessions of faith. Now I would like to say that there is one difference that I can see between the neo-Calvinist movement and the other four... it can more widely claim to be endemic [peculiar to a particular locality or people] to the Baptist past, the Baptist heritage and teaching of the past, than can the other four. What I am saying is that whether we want to be Calvinists or not today any serious study of our Baptist past must acknowledge that Baptists have been Calvinists [brackets mine].[2]

Lest you think this is a biased view, here is a quote from the Encyclopedia Britannica on the doctrinal history of Baptists:

> *Doctrine.* History. Initially, Baptists were characterized theologically by strong to moderate Calvinism. The dominant continuing tradition in both England and the United States was Particular Baptist. By 1800 this older tradition was beginning to be replaced by evangelical doctrines fashioned by the leaders of the evangelical revival in England and the Great Awakening in America and further elaborated by subsequent New England divines and frontier revivalists. By 1900 the older Calvinism had almost completely disappeared, and Evangelicalism was dominant. The conciliatory tendency of Evangelicalism and its almost complete preoccupation with heart-religion and the conversion experience largely denuded it of any solid theological structure opening the door to a new theological current, which in its later phases became known as Modernism. Modernism, which was an attempt to adjust the Christian faith to the new intellectual climate, made large inroads among the Baptists of England and the United States during the first two decades of the 20th century, and Baptists provided many outstanding leaders of the move-

---

[2] Quoted in E. C. Reisinger, *Reforming A Local Church* (Pensecola, FL: Chapel Library, n.d.), 2–3.

ment, including Shailer Mathews and Harry Emerson Fosdick. To many, these views seemed to pose a threat to the uniqueness of the Christian revelation, and they precipitated a counterreaction that became known as Fundamentalism (a movement emphasizing biblical literalism). As a result of the controversy that followed, many Baptists developed a distaste for theology and became content to find their unity as Baptists in promoting denominational enterprises. By 1950 both Modernists and Fundamentalists were becoming disenchanted with the positions into which they had been forced in the heat of controversy and it was from among adherents of both camps that a more creative theological encounter began to take place. While the majority of Baptists remained non-theological in their interests and concerns, there were multiplying signs that Baptist leadership was increasingly recognizing the necessity for renewed theological inquiry.[3]

Many advise against using the term "Calvinism" because it is such a red-flag word. There are several erroneous impressions about what Calvinism teaches. Some associate Calvinism with infant damnation, no free will and a lack of evangelism and missions. These impressions create all sorts of confusion and even hostility. Professor Ben Warburton in his book entitled *Calvinism* was correct when he said,

> To mention it before some, is like shaking the proverbial red flag before an enraged bull. It arouses the fiercest passions of their nature, and brings forth a torrent of abuse and calumny. But, because men have fought against it, or because they hate it, or perhaps misunderstand it, is no reason or logical cause why we should turn the doctrine adrift, or cast it behind our backs. The real question, the all-important question, is not: How do men receive it? but, Is it true?[4]

I do agree that the term itself should be used discretely. We must be careful, however, to define it properly. For this reason I want to give a brief historical review so that the tremendous contribution of Calvinism to church history and especially Southern Baptist history can be seen and hopefully better understood.

---

[3] New Encyclopedia Britannica, 15th ed. (1980), S.V. "Baptists."
[4] Warburton, Ben A. *Calvinism* (Grand Rapids, MI: Eerdmans, 1955), 23.

An Overview of Calvinism

Calvinism is the teaching of the Bible. It is the gospel of our Lord Jesus Christ in all its purity. One of C. H. Spurgeon's statements about it summarizes my thoughts,

> It is no novelty, then, that I am preaching; no new doctrine. I love to proclaim these strong old doctrines, that are called by nickname Calvinism, but which are surely and verily the revealed truth of God as it is in Christ Jesus. By this truth I make a pilgrimage into [the] past, and as I go, I see father after father, confessor after confessor, martyr after martyr, standing up to shake hands with me… taking these things to be the standard of my faith, I see the land of the ancients peopled with my brethren; I behold multitudes who confess the same as I do, and acknowledge that this is the religion of God's own church.[5]

Its Significance in Church History

Loraine Boettner champions Calvinism when he says in his classic book, *The Reformed Doctrine of Predestination*,

> Among the past and present advocates of these doctrines are to be found some of the world's greatest and wisest men. It was taught not only by Calvin, but by Luther, Zwingli, Melanchton… by Bullinger, Bucer, and all of the outstanding leaders in the Reformation. While differing on some other points they agreed on this doctrine of Predestination and taught it with emphasis. Luther's chief work, "The Bondage of the Will" shows that he went into the doctrine as heartily as did Calvin himself…. The Puritans in England and those who early settled in America, as well as the Covenanters in Scotland and the Huguenots in France, were thorough-going Calvinists; and it is little credit to historians in general that this fact has been so largely passed over in silence…. The great majority of the creeds of historic Christendom have set forth the doctrines of Election, Predestination, and final Perseverance, as will readily be seen by any one who will make even a cursory study of the subject. On the other hand Arminianism existed for centuries only as a heresy on the outskirts of true religion, and in fact it was not championed by an organized Christian church until the year 1784, at which time it was incorporated

---

[5] Quoted in David N. Steele and Curtis C. Thomas, *The Five Points of Calvinism*, (Phillipsburg, NJ: Presbyterian and Reformed Publishing, 1963), 8.

into the system of doctrine of the Methodist Church of England. The great theologians of history, Augustine, Wycliff, Luther, Calvin, Zwingli, Zanchius, Owen, Whitefield, Toplady, and in more recent times Hodge, Dabney, Cunningham, Smith, Shedd, Warfield, and Kuyper, held this doctrine and taught it with force. That they have been the lights and ornaments of the highest type of Christianity will be admitted by practically all Protestants. Furthermore, their works on this great subject have never been answered.... From the time of the Reformation up until about one hundred years ago these doctrines were boldly set forth by the great majority of the ministers and teachers in the Protestant churches; but today we find far the greater majority holding and teaching other systems. It is only rarely that we now come across those who can be called "Calvinists without reserve".... The tendency in our enlightened age is to look upon Calvinism as a worn-out and obsolete creed.[6]

Floyd E. Hamilton says,

The average church member, or even minister of the gospel, is inclined to look upon a person who declares that he believes in Predestination, with a glance of amused tolerance. It seems incredible to them that there should exist such an intellectual curiosity as a real Calvinist, in an age of enlightenment like the present. As for seriously examining the arguments for Calvinism, the idea never enters their heads. It is deemed as out of date as the Inquisition, or the idea of a flat world, and is looked upon as one of the fantastic schemes of thought that men held before the age of modern science.[7]

Regardless of how men may evaluate it, it has yet to be disproved from Scripture. Countless people have tried but can only disagree at best, and that without any real scriptural basis.

Calvinism has been largely ignored or dismissed in our day. I am amazed at the number of people I talk to who misunderstand the doctrines or are indifferent to studying the doctrines. Many have never given the doctrines of grace a thorough, prayerful and fair examination.

---

[6] Loraine Boettner, *The Reformed Doctrine of Predestination* (Phillipsburg, NJ: Presbyterian and Reformed Publishing, 1932), 1–3.

[7] Floyd E. Hamilton, "The Reformed Faith in the Modern World" (Sovereign Grace Union, 1949), quoted in Boettner, *Reformed Doctrine of Predestination*, 2.

Calvin himself studied Scripture until the following statement could be said about him,

> It was Calvin who wrought out this system of theological thought with such logical clearness and emphasis that it has ever since borne his name. He did not, of course, originate the system but only set forth what appeared to him to shine forth so clearly from the pages of Holy Scripture. Augustine had taught the essentials of the system a thousand years before Calvin was born, and the whole body of the leaders of the Reformation movement taught the same. But it was given to Calvin with his deep knowledge of Scripture, his keen intellect and systematizing genius, to set forth and defend these truths more clearly and ably than had ever been done before.[8]

Anyone who has studied the life of John Calvin must admit that he was not infallible. He certainly had his shortcomings. However, it is not fair to dismiss the entire system of theology that bears his name because he had certain discrepancies in his character or was not correct in every point of his theology.

My first impression of John Calvin was when I attended a Methodist college. I remember sitting in class one day and listening to a professor quote a little jingle about Calvin. It went like this:

> Ding Dong Bell
> Babies in Hell
> Who Put Them In
> John Cal - vin

Did Calvin really believe babies were sentenced to hell? I visualized him as stern, out of touch and unbiblical, who believed in a cruel, capricious, monster of a God. Since then, I have obviously come to see him as a very godly and remarkably gifted man. Any honest evaluation of his theology must at least be respected, whether one agrees with him or not. To be a Calvinist does not mean one has to completely agree with him. I am not ashamed to be called a Calvinist. I only wish the term could be used with greater understanding and appreciation.

---

[8] Boettner, *Reformed Doctrine of Predestination*, 4.

The Cannons of Dort 1618–1619

It is essential to delve into the origin and content of the famous Five Points of Calvinism and Arminianism in order to define terms and give greater clarity. These two opposing systems must be understood in order to gain a proper perspective. Thus I give you, from the pen of Steele and Thomas, a brief historical overview of their formation in Holland at the Synod of Dort in 1618–1619.

> In 1610, just one year after the death of James Arminius (a Dutch seminary professor) five articles of faith based on his teachings were drawn up by his followers. The Arminians, as his followers came to be called, presented these five doctrines to the State of Holland in the form of a "Remonstrance" (i.e., a protest). The Arminian party insisted that the *Belgic Confession of Faith* and the *Heidelberg Catechism* (the official expression of the doctrinal position of the Churches of Holland) be changed to conform to the doctrinal views contained in the Remonstrance. The Arminians objected to those doctrines upheld in both the catechism and the confession relating to divine sovereignty, human inability, unconditional election or predestination, particular redemption, irresistible grace, and the perseverance of the saints. It was in connection with these matters that they wanted the official standards of the Church of Holland revised.
>
> A national Synod was called to meet in Dort in 1618 for the purpose of examining the views of Arminius in the light of Scripture. The Great Synod was convened by the States—General of Holland on November 13, 1618. There were 84 members and 18 secular commissioners. Included were 27 delegates from Germany, the Palatinate, Switzerland and England. There were 154 sessions held during the seven months that the Synod met to consider these matters, the last of which was on May 9, 1619.[9]

This Synod unanimously rejected the Arminian system and declared it to be heresy. Just to reject Arminianism was not enough for this great body of divines. The "Five Points of Calvinism" were systematized after having long been believed and espoused in church history.

---

[9] Material reproduced by permission of Presbyterian and Reformed Publishing, Steele and Thomas, *Five Points*, 13–14.

No doubt it will seem strange to many in our day that the Synod of Dort rejected as heretical the five doctrines advanced by the Arminians, for these doctrines have gained wide acceptance in the modern Church. In fact, they are seldom questioned in our generation. But the vast majority of the Protestant theologians of that day took a much different view of the matter. They maintained that the Bible set forth a system of doctrine quite different from that advocated by the Arminian party. Salvation was viewed by the members of the Synod as a work of grace from beginning to end; in no sense did they believe that the sinner saved himself or contributed to his salvation. Adam's fall had completely ruined the race. All men were by nature spiritually dead and their wills were in bondage to sin and Satan. The ability to believe the gospel was itself a gift from God, bestowed only upon those whom He had chosen to be the objects of His unmerited favor. It was not man, but God, who determined which sinners would be shown mercy and saved. This, in essence, is what the members of the Synod of Dort understood the Bible to teach.[10]

Lest the contemporary relevance of this Synod be minimized, even though it took place over 400 years ago, take note of the following significant statement written in *To Whom He Will*, a book published by the Reformed Literature Information Society:

The Arminian error, though it bears a seventeenth century name, is as old as man, and crops up again and again, often in new forms, even in evangelical dress. It is to be found now amongst those Christians, who, while they profess biblical doctrine, yet insist upon the *ability* of man to choose God for himself. It is also current, in far more radical form among the great number of the neo-orthodox and liberal theologians who concentrate upon anthropology in their thinking and substitute for the Reformation quest after a gracious God, they quest instead after a gracious neighbor.

It is to be found wherever men do not in humility, obedience and faith, subject themselves to the God of the Scriptures, and ascribe to Him, not only the initiative, but also all the means and the fulfillment of salvation in every part. The fundamental truth which Dort held high is the truth for which the Reformation, in the line of Augustine and the Word of God itself, firmly stood. *Soli Dei Gloria*.[11]

---

[10] Ibid., 15.

[11] *To Whom He Will* (Nundah, Queensland: Reformed Literature Information Society, n.d.), 5.

The Five Points of Arminianism and Calvinism

Steele and Thomas have provided one of the most helpful presentations contrasting the two views of Calvinism and Arminianism. I quote their comparison at length:

The "Five Points" Of Arminianism:

(1) Free Will or Human Ability

Although human nature was seriously affected by the fall, man has not been left in a state of total spiritual helplessness. God graciously enables every sinner to repent and believe, but He does so in such a manner as not to interfere with man's freedom. Each sinner possesses a free will, and his eternal destiny depends on how he uses it. Man's freedom consists of his ability to choose good over evil in spiritual matters; his will is not enslaved to his sinful nature. The sinner has the power to either cooperate with God's spirit and be regenerated or resist God's grace and perish. The lost sinner needs the Spirit's assistance, but he does not have to be regenerated by the Spirit before he can believe, for faith is man's act and precedes the new birth. Faith is the sinner's gift to God; it is man's contribution to salvation.

(2) Conditional Election

God's choice of certain individuals unto salvation before the foundation of the world was based upon His foreseeing that they would respond to His call. He selected only those whom He knew would of themselves freely believe the gospel. Election therefore was determined by or conditioned upon what man would do. The faith which God foresaw and upon which He based His choice was not given to the sinner by God (it was not reacted by the regenerating power of the Holy Spirit) but resulted solely from man's will. It was left entirely up to man as to who would believe and therefore as to who would be elected unto salvation. God chose those whom He knew would, of their own free will, choose Christ. Thus the sinner's choice of Christ, not God's choice of the sinner, is the ultimate cause of salvation.

(3) Universal Redemption or General Atonement

Christ's redeeming work made it possible for everyone to be saved but did not actually secure the salvation of anyone. Although Christ died for all men and for every man, only those who believe in Him are saved. His death enabled God to pardon sinners on the condition that they believe, but it did not actually put away anyone's sins. Christ's redemption becomes effective only if man chooses to accept it.

(4) The Holy Spirit Can Be Effectually Resisted

The Spirit calls inwardly all those who are called outwardly by the gospel invitation; He does all that He can to bring every sinner to salvation. But inasmuch as man is free, he can successfully resist the Spirit's call. The Spirit cannot regenerate the sinner until he believes; faith (which is man's contribution) precedes and makes possible the new birth. Thus, man's free will limits the Spirit in the application of Christ's saving work. The Holy Spirit can only draw to Christ those who allow Him to have His way with them. Until the sinner responds, the Spirit cannot give life. God's grace, therefore, is not invincible; it can be, and often is, resisted and thwarted by man.

(5) Falling from Grace

Those who believe and are truly saved can lose their salvation by failing to keep up their faith, etc. All Arminians have not been agreed on this point; some have held that believers are eternally secure in Christ—that once a sinner is regenerated, he can never be lost.

According to Arminianism:

Salvation is accomplished through the combined efforts of God (who takes the initiative) and man (who must respond)—man's response being the determining factor. God has provided salvation for everyone, but His provision becomes effective only for those who, of their own free will, "choose" to cooperate with Him and accept His offer of grace. At the crucial point, man's will plays a decisive role; thus man, not God, determines who will be the recipients of the gift of salvation.

Rejected by the Synod of Dort

This was the system of thought contained in the "Remonstrance" (though the "five points" were not originally arranged in this order). It was submitted by the Arminians to the Church of Holland in 1610 for adoption but was rejected by the Synod of Dort in 1619 on the ground that it was unscriptural.

The "Five Points" Of Calvinism:

(1) Total Inability or Total Depravity

Because of the fall, man is unable of himself to savingly believe the gospel. The sinner is dead, blind, and deaf to the things of God; his heart is deceitful and desperately corrupt. His will is not free, it is in bondage to his evil nature, therefore, he will not—indeed he cannot—choose good over evil in the spiritual realm. Consequently, it takes much more than the Spirit's assistance to bring a sinner to Christ—it takes regeneration by which the Spirit makes the sinner alive and gives him a new nature. Faith is not something man contributes to salvation but is itself a part of God's gift of salvation—it is God's gift to the sinner, not the sinner's gift to God.

(2) Unconditional Election

God's choice of certain individuals unto salvation before the foundation of the world rested solely in His own sovereign will. His choice of particular sinners was not based on any foreseen response or obedience on their part, such as faith, repentance, etc. On the contrary, God gives faith and repentance to each individual whom He selected. These acts are the result, not the cause of God's choice. Election therefore was not determined by or conditioned upon any virtuous quality or act foreseen in man. Those whom God sovereignly elected He brings through the power of the Spirit to a willing acceptance of Christ. Thus God's choice of the sinner, not the sinner's choice of Christ, is the ultimate cause of salvation.

(3) Particular Redemption or Limited Atonement

Christ's redeeming work was intended to save the elect only and actually secured salvation for them. His death was a substitutionary endurance of the penalty of sin in the place of certain specified sinners. In addition to putting away the sins of His people, Christ's redemption secured everything necessary for their salvation, including faith which unites them to Him. The gift of faith is infallibly applied by the Spirit to all for whom Christ died, thereby guaranteeing their salvation.

(4) The Efficacious Call of the Spirit or Irresistible Grace.

In addition to the outward general call to salvation which is made to everyone who hears the gospel, the Holy Spirit extends to the elect a special inward call that inevitably brings them to salvation. The external call (which is made to all without distinction) can be, and often is, rejected; whereas the internal call (which is made only to the elect) cannot be rejected; it always results in conversion. By means of this special call the Spirit irresistibly draws sinners to Christ. He is not limited in His work of applying salvation by man's will, nor is He dependent upon man's cooperation for success. The Spirit graciously causes the elect sinner to cooperate, to believe, to repent, to come freely and willingly to Christ.

God's grace, therefore, is invincible; it never fails to result in the salvation of those to whom it is extended.

(5) Perseverance of the Saints

All who were chosen by God, redeemed by Christ, and given faith by the Spirit are eternally saved. They are kept in faith by the power of Almighty God and thus persevere to the end.

According to Calvinism:

Salvation is accomplished by the almighty power of the Triune God. The Father chose a people, the Son died for them, the Holy Spirit makes Christ's death effective by bringing the elect to faith and repentance, thereby causing them to willingly obey the gospel. The entire process (election, redemption, regeneration) is the work of God and is by grace alone. Thus God, not man, determines who will be the recipients of the gift of salvation.

Reaffirmed by the Synod of Dort

This system of theology was reaffirmed by the Synod of Dort in 1619 as the doctrine of salvation contained in the Holy Scriptures. The system was at that time formulated into "five points" (in answer to the five points submitted by the Arminians) and has ever since been known as "the five points of Calvinism." [12]

It is important to be reminded at this point that Calvinism or the doctrines of grace are not restricted to these Five Points. They are certainly an integral part but by no means do they teach all that Calvinism teaches. Actually Calvinism has thousands of points. It is a by-word for biblical, orthodox, historic Christianity. Whatever the Bible teaches about salvation is what Calvinism teaches—no more, no less. It is a slogan that represents correct theology. Whatever the Bible teaches about God, Christ, the Holy Spirit, justification, sanctification, adoption, etc. is what Calvinism teaches.

[12] Reproduced by permission of P&R Publishing, *The Five Points of Calvinism: Defined, Defended and Documented*, David N. Steele and Curtis C. Thomas (Phillipsburg, NJ: P&R Publishing, 1963), 16–20. This comparison between Calvinism and Arminianism first appeared as a chart in an appendix in *Romans: An Interpretive Outline* by Steele and Thomas (Philadelphia, PA: Presbyterian and Reformed, 1963). Soon after the publication of the outline on Romans, the appendix was expanded into a book, *The Five Points of Calvinism* (1963, updated and expanded in 2004).

To narrow its meaning to less than that is to misrepresent it. In much the same way that the name Newton is associated with the law of gravity or Columbus with the discovery of America or Einstein with the Theory of Relativity, Calvin is associated with theology. He did not invent anything. He simply discovered, articulated and systematized biblical theology more ably and eloquently than anyone of his day. For that reason his name has since been attached to sound theology.

True Calvinism Equals Pure Grace

When all the caricatures are swept aside and Calvinism is seen for what it really is, it equals grace, pure grace, only grace, always grace and nothing but grace. It gives all glory to God and none to men. It honors God as the only Source of salvation. In this the Reformers were agreed. In their introduction to Luther's *Bondage of the Will*, J. I. Packer and O. R. Johnston draw this conclusion:

> Historically, it is a simple matter of fact that Martin Luther and John Calvin, and for that matter, Ulrich Zwingli, Martin Bucer, and all the leading Protestant theologians of the first epoch of the Reformation, stood on precisely the same ground here. On other points, they had their differences; but in asserting the helplessness of man in sin, and the sovereignty of God in grace, they were entirely at one. To all of them, these doctrines were the very life-blood of the Christian faith.[13]

One of the most helpful essays ever written to define true Calvinism is the introduction by J. I. Packer to John Owen's *Death of Death in the Death of Christ*. Owens' work is a deep mine of spiritual wealth, but it is worth the price of the book simply to read Packer's introduction. He explains as follows the contract between Calvinism and Arminianism:

> First, it should be observered that the "five points of Calvinism," so-called, are simply the Calvinistic answer to a five-point manifesto (the Remonstrance) put out by certain "Belgic semi-Pelagians" in the early seventeenth century. The theology which it contained (known to history as Arminianism) stemmed from two philosophical principles: first, that

---

[13] J. I Packer and O. R. Johnston, "Historical and Theological Introduction," in Martin Luther, *Bondage of the Will*, trans. J. I Packer and O. R. Johnston (Grand Rapids, MI: Fleming H. Revell, 1957), 58.

divine sovereignty is not compatible with human freedom, nor therefore with human responsibility; second, that ability limits obligation. (The charge of semi-Pelagianism was thus fully justified.) From these principles, the Arminian drew two deductions: first, that since the Bible regards faith as a free and responsible human act, it cannot be caused by God, but is exercised independently of Him; second, that since the Bible regards faith as obligatory on the part of all who hear the gospel, ability to believe must be universal. Hence, they maintained, Scripture must be interpreted as teaching the following positions: (1) Man is never so completely corrupted by sin that he cannot savingly believe the gospel when it is put before him, nor (2) is he ever so completely controlled by God that he cannot reject it. (3) God's election of those who shall be saved is prompted by His foreseeing that they will of their own accord believe. (4) Christ's death did not ensure the salvation of anyone for it did not secure the gift of faith to anyone (there is no such gift); what it did was rather to create a possibility of salvation for everyone if they believe. (5) It rests with believers to keep themselves in a state of grace by keeping up their faith; those who fail here fall away and are lost. Thus Arminianism made man's salvation depend ultimately on man himself, saving faith being viewed throughout as man's own work and, because his own, not God's in him.

The Synod of Dort was convened in 1618 to pronounce on this theology, and the "five points of Calvinism" represent its counter-affirmations. They stem from a very different principle—the biblical principle that "salvation is of the Lord" [Jonah 2:9]; and they may be summarized thus: (1) Fallen man in his natural state lacks all power to believe the gospel, just as he lacks all power to believe the law, despite all external inducements that may be extended to him. (2) God's election is a free, sovereign, unconditional choice of sinners, as sinners, to be redeemed by Christ, given faith and brought to glory. (3) The redeeming work of Christ had as its end and goal the salvation of the elect. (4) The work of the Holy Spirit in bringing men to faith never fails to achieve its objective. (5) Believers are kept in faith and grace by the unconquerable power of God till they come to glory. These give points are conveniently denoted by the mnemonic TULIP: Total depravity, Unconditional election, Limited atonement, Irresistible grace, Preservation of the saints.

Now here are two coherent interpretations of the biblical gospel, which stand in evident opposition to each other. The difference between them (Calvinism and Arminianism) is not primarily one of emphasis, but of content. One proclaims a God who saves; the other speaks of a God Who enables man to save himself. One view (Calvinism) presents the three great acts of the Holy Trinity for the recovering of lost mankind—election by the Father, redemption by the Son, calling by the Spirit—as directed towards the same persons, and as securing their salvation infallibly. The other view (Arminianism) gives each act a different reference (the objects of redemption being all mankind, of calling, those who hear the gospel, and of election, those hearers who respond), and denies that any man's salvation is secured by any of them. The two theologies thus conceive the plan of salvation in quite different terms. One makes salvation depend on the work of God, the other on a work of man; one regards faith as part of God's gift of salvation, the other as man's own contribution to salvation; one gives all the glory of saving believers to God, the other divides the praise between God, Who, so to speak, built the machinery of salvation, and man, who by believing operated it. Plainly, these differences are important, and the permanent value of the 'five points,' as a summary of Calvinism, is that they make clear the points at which, and the extent to which, these two conceptions are at variance.[14]

Packer goes on to clarify that the "five points" came about historically as a response to the "five points" in the Remonstrance. In reality, Calvinism is one point:

For the five points, though separately stated, are really inseparable. They hang together; you cannot reject one without rejecting them all, at least in the sense in which the Synod meant them. For to Calvinism there is really only *one* point to be made in the field of soteriology: the point that *God saves sinners*. *God*—the Triune Jehovah, Father, Son and Spirit; three Persons working together in sovereign wisdom, power and love to achieve the salvation of a chosen people, the Father electing, the Son fulfilling the Father's will by redeeming, the Spirit executing the purpose of Father and Son by renewing. *Saves*—does everything, first to last, that is involved in bringing man from death in sin to life in glory: plans, achieves and communicates redemption, calls and keeps, justifies, sanctifies, glorifies. *Sinners*—men as God finds them, guilty, vile, helpless, powerless, unable to lift a finger to do God's will or better their spiritual lot. *God saves sinners*—and the force of this confession may not be weakened by disrupting the unity of the work of the Trinity, or by dividing the achievement of salvation between God and man and making the decisive part man's own, or by soft-pedalling the sinner's inability so as to allow him to share the praise of his salvation with his Saviour. This is the one point of Calvinistic soteriology which the "five points" are concerned to establish and Arminianism in all its forms to deny: namely, that sinners

---

[14] J. I. Packer, "Introductory Essay" in John Owen, *Death of Death in the Death of Christ* (Edinburgh: The Banner of Truth, 1967), 3–5.

do not save themselves in any sense at all, but that salvation, first and last, whole and entire, past, present and future, is of the Lord, to whom be glory for ever; amen.[15]

True Calvinism then readily confesses that our only hope is in God and God alone. It sees the desperate, helpless state of man in his sin and the amazing, gracious provision of God in sending His Son to die on the cross for sinners and it declares that all glory belongs to God. Packer concludes:

> Now the real nature of Calvinistic soteriology becomes plain. It is no artificial oddity, nor a product of over-bold logic. Its central confession, that *God saves sinners*, that *Christ redeemed us by His blood*, is the witness both of the Bible and of the believing heart. The Calvinist is the Christian who confesses before men in his theology just what he believes in his heart before God when he prays. He thinks and speaks at all times of the sovereign grace of God in the way every Christian does when he pleads for the souls of others, or when he obeys the impulse of worship which rises unbidden within him, prompting him to deny himself all praise and to give all glory of his salvation to his Saviour."[16]

We can plainly see from these enlightening facts that we owe no small debt to Calvinists both historically as well as theologically.

[15] Ibid., 6.
[16] Ibid., 10.

3

Significant Shapers, Founders and Leaders of the Southern Baptist Convention

Now I wish to show the significant role Calvinists have played in shaping Southern Baptist history. It sounds like a theological symphony to hear some of the abiding voices of our Baptist past. It is a virtual Calvinistic hall of fame. Ponder the following facts about some of these people and take special notice that each one held very strongly to the doctrines of grace: Roger Williams (1603–1684) was a Baptist for a short time and he defended religious liberty on the basis of his Calvinistic theology. Obadiah Holmes (1607–1682) was a leading Baptist with strong Calvinistic beliefs. Benjamin Keach was one of the framers of the *London Confession of Faith* of 1689, adopted by Baptists in America in 1742 as the *Philadelphia Confession of Faith*. It is amazing indeed to study how the great truths of our faith are beautifully systematized therein.

I consider C. H. Spurgeon as probably the greatest preacher since New Testament times. He pastored the famous Metropolitan Tabernacle in London for many years and is called "the Prince of Preachers." His thousands of published sermons and books serve as one of the richest Christian libraries available in history. He thundered forth the doctrines of grace in a masterful way. In a sermon on Matthew 24:24 he makes this statement:

> I do not hesitate to say, that next to the doctrine of the crucifixion and the resurrection of our blessed Lord—no doctrine had such prominence in the early Christian church as the doctrine of the election of Grace.[17]

[17] C. H. Spurgeon, "Effects of Sound Doctrine" Sermon 324 (April 22, 1860) in *The New Park Street Pulpit*, vol. 6 (Pasadena, TX: Pilgrim Publications, 1981), 301–302.

On another occasion he said:

> There seem to be an inveterate prejudice in the human mind against this doctrine, and although most other doctrines will be received by professing Christians, some with caution, others with pleasure, yet this one seems to be most frequently disregarded and discarded.[18]

Issac Backus (1724–1806) was a very influential early Baptist preacher who defended Calvinism. Andrew Fuller (1754–1815) helped form the Baptist Missionary Society in 1792. William Carey (1761–1834), a Calvinist, helped start the modern missionary movement and is considered "The Father of Modern Missions." The missionary zeal of this man and many others defies the false idea that Calvinism is anti-missions. Luther Rice (1783–1836) founded the "General Missionary Convention of the Baptist Denomination of the United States of America for Foreign Missions." A seminary that was established in Jacksonville, Florida bears his name. Adoniram Judson (1788–1850) carried the gospel of God's sovereign grace as a missionary to Burma. Frances Wayland (1796–1865) was an outstanding educator and president of Brown University. Basil Manly, Sr. (1798–1868) and his son Basil Manly, Jr.(1825–1892) were both significant founders and leaders of the SBC. Even Lottie Moon, after whom our SBC foreign missions offering is named, in her life and ministry gives evidence of believing the doctrines of grace.

The first presidents of the SBC firmly held to the doctrines of grace. They were, W. B. Johnson (first president from 1845 to 1850), R. B. C. Howell (second president from 1851 to 1858) and Richard Fuller (third president from 1859 to 1864). P. H. Mell was president for seventeen years (1861–1871 and 1879–1887) and held more official positions in SBC life than any other Southern Baptist in its history. He authored *Predestination and the Saints' Perseverance*, one of the most helpful books available on the subject.[19]

J. L. Dagg has to be considered one of our most influential leaders because of his monumental theological work entitled *Manual of Theology*.[20]

---

[18] C. H. Spurgeon, "Election" Sermon 41 (September 2, 1855) in *The New Park Street Pulpit*, vol. 1 (Pasadena, TX: Pilgrim Publications, 1981), 311.

[19] P. H. Mell, *Predestination and the Saints' Perseverance* (Charleston, SC: Southern Baptist Publication Society, 1851).

[20] John L. Dagg, *Manual of Theology* (Charleston, SC: Southern Baptist Publication Society, 1857).

J. P. Boyce was the primary founder and first president of the Southern Baptist Theological Seminary in Louisville, the first Southern Baptist seminary. His theological work entitled *Abstract of Systematic Theology* is classic. He held to the following definition of election as given in the *Abstract of Principles*:

> Election is God's eternal choice of some persons unto everlasting life—not because of foreseen merit in them, but of his mere mercy in Christ—in consequence of which choice they are called, justified and glorified.[21]

John A. Broadus (1827–1895) assisted in establishing Southern Seminary and was a mighty preacher of the gospel. His book *The Preparation and Delivery of Sermons* is probably the most studied book on the subject of any other among Southern Baptist ministers.[22] Dr. Broadus said of election, "From the divine side, we see that the Scriptures teach an eternal election of men to eternal life simply out of God's good pleasure."[23]

B. H. Carroll (1843–1914) was the founder and first president of the Southwestern Baptist Theological Seminary in Ft. Worth. His most famous work was his set of commentaries entitled *An Interpretation of the English Bible*. In his day, the doctrines of grace were faithfully taught at the seminary.

Other men, such as William Williams, E. C. Dargan and F. H. Kerfoot of Southern Seminary, all very active in significant leadership positions in Southern Baptist life, held firmly to sovereign grace. W. T. Conner, long time professor at Southwestern Seminary was one of the last prominent Calvinistic Southern Baptist voices to be heard. J. B. Gambrell, president of the SBC from 1917 to 1920 and editor of both the *Texas Baptist Standard* and the *Mississippi Baptist Record* at the same time, was staunch in his belief about unconditional election and predestination.

Speaking of Mississippi, it is of particular interest to me, being a former Mississippi Baptist, that early Baptists there were strongly Calvinistic.

---

[21] J. P. Boyce, *Abstract of Systematic Theology* (Philadelphia: American Baptist Publication Society, 1887; reprint ed., Cape Coral, FL: Founders Press, 2006), 513.

[22] John A. Broadus, *Preparation and Delivery of Sermons* (1870, revised ed., NY: Hodder and Stoughton, 1898).

[23] John Broadus, quoted in Ernest Reisinger, *A Southern Baptist Looks at the Biblical Doctrine of Election* (Cape Coral, FL: Founders Press, 2000), 15.

The following statement was written by Baptists near Natchez in October, 1791:

> We do fully believe ... the doctrines of particular redemption, person-
> al election, effectual call, justification by the imputed righteousness of
> Christ, pardon of sin by atoning blood, believer's baptism by immersion,
> the final perseverance of the saints, the resurrection of the dead, and eter-
> nal judgment.[24]

Also, as Director of Missions for the Bryan Baptist Association, I was quite interested to review a book about the history of our Association entitled *Co-Operating Churches Under God*. The 12 Articles of Faith that was the doctrinal statement in the beginning years of our Association, known as the Bethel Association in 1897, was strongly Calvinistic. Articles 3–8 read as follows:

> Belief in... the doctrine of eternal and particular election... in the doc-
> trine of original sin... in man's impotency to recover himself from the
> fallen state he is in by nature, by his own free will and ability... that sin-
> ners are justified in the sight of God only by the imputed righteousness
> of Christ... that God's elect shall be called, renewed and sanctified by
> the Holy Spirit...that saints shall persevere in grace and never fully fall
> away.[25]

Upon investigation, it is no surprise that similar statements of faith can easily be found in many church, association and state convention archives. It is interesting to learn that the name Broadman, trade name of the general book publishing enterprise Broadman Press, of the Sunday School Board of the SBC (now LifeWay), was coined by book editor John Leonard Hill from the last names of John Albert Broadus and Basil Manly, Jr., both strong Calvinists.

It was amid the strong leadership of our founders that the great SBC mission efforts were born. Evangelism and missions were not killed, or even hindered. They were undergirded with correct biblical emphasis. In no way did these people display a cold or indifferent Christianity. They

---

[24] R. A. McLemore, *A History of Mississippi Baptists, 1780–1970*. (Jackson, MS: Mississippi Baptist Convention Board, 1971), 14.

[25] Erma Leigh Taylor, *Co–operating Churches under God*. (Durant, OK: Published by Author, 1976), 6.

were militantly aggressive in building churches and taking the gospel to the ends of the earth. They were warm-hearted, godly people who whole-heartedly loved Christ and His Word. They were outstanding evangelists and soul winners. They did not practice shallow or sub-biblical methods. They had tremendous insight and understanding of the gospel and the mission of the Church. May God help us to pick up the mantle they gave us, which, in many respects has been dropped, and continue in their tradition today.

I am thrilled that outstanding men such as Dr. Al Mohler, current president of the Southern Baptist Theological Seminary, are leading us back to our theological roots. Dr. Mohler's commitment to the founding principles of the Seminary is quite well known. From its beginning to this very day, every faculty member has signed the Seminary's Calvinistic doctrinal statement, the *Abstract of Principles*, Southern Baptists' first recognized confession of faith. Southeastern Baptist Theological Seminary in Wake Forest, North Carolina also requires its faculty to sign the *Abstract of Principles* along with the *Baptist Faith and Message*.

In light of our rich history we must ask, what has caused us to become so seriously detached from our theological roots? It certainly didn't happen overnight. There was a gradual drifting away. Dr. Tom Nettles writes,

> ... both negligence and rejection have taken their toll upon the Baptist understanding of and—even more—commitment to those truths that Baptists once held dear.[26]

Dr. Nettles continues:

> This consensus in the doctrines of grace was perpetuated in Southern Baptist life through the second decade of the present century....
> This virtually unanimous belief disintegrated along the way. Among several contributing factors, most prominent from a content standpoint, were the theological methodology of E. Y. Mullins and the evangelistic methodology of L. R. Scarborough, presidents of Southern Seminary and Southwestern Seminary respectively.... Vestiges of the old doctrines still remained in places, as in the teaching and writing of W.T. Conner, of Southwestern Seminary (especially the doctrine of election) and in the faithful ministry of J.B. Tidwell at Baylor University. With ever-increas-

---

[26] Thomas Nettles, *By His Grace and For His Glory* (Grand Rapids, MI: Baker, 1986; revised ed., Cape Coral, FL: Founders Press, 2006), x.

ing rapidity, however, concerns focused more and more on denominational programs that minimized and streamlined doctrinal materials. The
doctrines were first ignored till they passed from the scene—and finally
were either opposed openly as destructive of true piety and mission zeal
or discussed as some idiosyncrasy of the past, to be recoiled from with
great horror.

Crises related to biblical authority, the necessity of the atonement,
and the uniqueness of Christianity as the way to God have come to
Southern Baptists only because the doctrines of God's sovereignty were
first jettisoned from their proper place as the fountainhead from which
all other doctrines receive their coherence.... Southern Baptists can only
expect further theological fragmentation unless God in his mercy grants
a Reformation comparable to that which occurred in sixteenth-century
Europe.

It is the prayer of this author that this denomination, which has
all the trappings of greatness, may escape the solemn reality graphically
pictured in our Lord's description of some in his day: whitewashed sep-
ulchers, clean and bright on the outside—but inside full of dead men's
bones.[27]

Something is definitely wrong when our Convention can boast of over
16,000,000 people but only about half can even be located. On top of
that, far less than half of those left can be considered active and faithful
members of their churches.[28] Many people have gotten into our churches
under false pretenses. There are tares among the wheat and wolves dressed
in sheep's clothing that are mixed in the sheepfold (Matthew 13:24–30;
7:15–20).

The current doctrinal statement of Southern Baptists is the *Baptist
Faith and Message*. The section entitled "God's Purpose of Grace" states:

> Election is the gracious purpose of God, according to which He regener-
> ates, sanctifies, and glorifies sinners. It is consistent with the free agency
> of man, and comprehends all the means in connection with the end. It
> is a glorious display of God's sovereign goodness, and is infinitely wise,
> holy, and unchangeable. It excludes boasting and promotes humility.[29]

[27] Ibid., xlvi–xlvii.

[28] According to the 2007 Southern Baptist Convention annual Church Profiles, there are 16,266,920 members in Southern Baptist Churches. Those same
profiles indicate that only 6,148,868 of those members attend a primary worship
service of their church in a typical week.

[29] *Baptist Faith and Message* (Nashville, TN: LifeWay Christian Resources,
2000), 12.

The *Baptist Faith and Message* was drawn from and based upon the *New Hampshire Confession of Faith* in 1925. In those days our Convention was still Calvinistic enough that this declaration of faith was understood to uphold sovereign grace. L. D. Cole writes:

> It is observed that the New Hampshire Confession is a Calvinistic confession in design and birth and recognized as such by all concerned well into this [20th]century.... It] is more of a working document that has rounded off some of the rough edges and set forth the faith in its simplest form.[30]

In an effort to "round off the rough edges and set forth the faith in its simplest form," the framers of this statement of faith added impetus to our Convention's already slow but sure drift away from its doctrinal roots. From the twenties to the eighties the precious truths of sovereign grace were virtually buried in a sea of doctrinal diversion, ignorance, neglect and indifference. A maze of denominational structuring took its place. In those years, with the exception of only a few, Calvinistic voices across our Convention were silenced. The doctrines of grace were lost in obscurity. When they were finally resurrected, they were thought to be anything but Southern Baptist. They have been shunned by some as outdated, divisive, impractical, unnecessary and even heretical.

Early Baptist confessions and statements of faith lead us to see the "ancient paths" that Jeremiah tells us to ask for. He admonished us to ask where the good way is, and walk in it. Only there will we find rest for our souls (Jeremiah 6:16).

At this point I must hasten to reiterate, lest I be misunderstood, that I am most grateful to be a part of the SBC. I am Southern Baptist to the bone. If you cut me I would "bleed Cooperative Program." I believe our programs and organizations are among the best. I admire our leadership and stand amazed that God has so richly blessed Southern Baptists with some of the most godly, gifted people to be found.

I am very committed to SBC life. My position as a Director of Missions affirms that. Southern Baptists have been used of the Lord to bring me to faith, nurture me, educate me, support me and provide a host of lifelong friends.

---

[30] L. D. Cole, *The Doctrines of Grace in the New Hampshire Confession of Faith* (Ottisville, MI: Baptist Book Trust, 1979), 13, 24.

Our Lord has used Southern Baptists in a most remarkable and unique way. We are among those who lead the way in evangelism, church planting and global outreach. My heart's desire is to see us recover the great biblical truths that shaped our denomination. I wish to play a part in helping fix the doctrinal cracks that have slowly formed in our foundation and to adjust our course. Continue to journey with me as I define what I mean.

Part Three

A Biblical Journey

34

The big question is biblical accuracy. It matters not about my testimony or that of Baptists if our doctrinal stance cannot pass the test of Scripture. I'm wasting your time and mine if all this is biblically unsound. However, my primary purpose, with the gracious help of the Lord, is to let the Bible speak. A thorough look at Scripture will give convincing evidence that salvation is altogether of sovereign grace.

4

The Sovereignty of God

My journey in grace accelerated rapidly when I began to understand the sovereignty of God. I will never forget the dramatic way the Bible took on new meaning. In all my training I had somehow missed this life-changing truth. I have come to see that this is the key to understanding all truth.

It is not a cold, stuffy subject of debate to be relegated only to an intellectual academic community. It is imminently practical and instructive. There is nothing that elicits deeper humility from man and gives God more glory. Of course, this subject is infinite beyond our understanding. On the other hand, God has been pleased to reveal this truth so that we, at least to a limited degree can understand and greatly benefit from it.

In 1 Chronicles 29:10–11, David gives a very clear definition to the sovereignty of God:

> Praise be to you O Lord, God of our father Israel, from everlasting to everlasting. Yours, O Lord, is the greatness and the power and the glory and the majesty and the splendor, for every thing in heaven and earth is yours. Yours, O Lord, is the kingdom; you are exalted as head over all.

Simply put, it means what Revelation 19:6 says, "Hallelujah! For our Lord God Almighty reigns." The Bible designates God as the Most High (Daniel 4:34). He is Creator, Owner and Sustainer of all things and rules with complete authority. There is nothing at anytime or in any realm that God does not control and preside over.

This attribute of God makes all the others possible. Love, for instance, may seem more important but without sovereignty, love could not be completely demonstrated. He could not exercise His omnipresence, omniscience or total freedom if He had to be subject to anything or anyone.

God, for example, may want to establish justice or holiness, but if He does not reign supreme then circumstances would surely thwart His efforts.

There are far more than just a few proof texts about God's sovereignty. This subject begins in Genesis and goes all the way through the Bible. It is the theme of Holy Writ. The first verse in the Bible affirms this when it says, "In the beginning God…"(Genesis 1:1). Isaiah 46:10–11 says "I make known the end from the beginning, from ancient times, what is still to come. I say: My purpose will stand, and I will do all that I please….What I have said, that will I bring about; what I have planned, that will I do."

God is infinitely elevated above the highest creature. He is Lord of heaven and earth. He is subject to none and He is swayed by none. He is completely independent, self-existent and self-sufficient. He has no needs, neither does He want for anything. He does as He pleases, only as He pleases and always as He pleases. None can stop or even slow Him down in the accomplishment of His eternal purpose. He is a law unto Himself.

From time to time we refer to God's plans. Actually He has only one plan. This He will infallibly accomplish. He has never had to call a heavenly conference and, in frustration change to "Plan B or C" because "Plan A" didn't work. There are never any surprises in heaven. God does not sit in heaven and wring His hands with worry wondering what to do. "In Him we were also chosen, having been predestined according to the plan of him who works out everything in conformity with the purpose of His will" (Ephesians 1:11). God does not anxiously wait to see what man will do and then act. A. W. Pink says,

> Is it not that a disappointed God is the One whom Christians believe in? From what is heard from the average evangelist today is not any serious hearer obliged to conclude that he professes to represent a God who is filled with benevolent intentions, yet unable to carry them out; that He is earnestly desirous of blessing men, but that they will not let Him? Then, must not the average hearer draw the inference that the Devil has gained the upper hand, and that God is to be pitied rather than blamed.[31]

This impression of God is what most seem to have. However, as Nebeuchadnezzar, the greatest monarch of his day discovered, after God humbled him with seven years of the worst kind of insanity, "His dominion is an eternal dominion; His kingdom endures from generation to gen-

---

[31] Pink, A. W., *The Sovereignty of God* (Grand Rapids, MI: Baker, 1930), 12.

eration. All the peoples of the earth are regarded as nothing. He does as He pleases with the powers of heaven and the peoples of the earth. No one can hold back His hand or say to Him: What have you done?" (Daniel 4:34–35).

Boettner says:

> The Arminian idea which assumes that the serious intentions of God may in some cases at least be defeated, and that man, who is not only a creature but a sinful creature, can exercise veto power over the plans of Almighty God, is in striking contrast with the Biblical idea of His immeasurable exaltation by which He is removed from all the weaknesses of humanity. That the plans of men are not always executed is due to a lack of power, or a lack of wisdom; but since God is unlimited in these and all other resources, no unforeseen emergencies can arise, and to Him the causes for change have no existence. To suppose that His plans fail and that He strives to no effect, is to reduce Him to the level of His creatures.[32]

"Our God is in heaven; he does whatever pleases him." (Psalm 115:3) The Most High God has no rival, is unlimited in power and glory, and is not affected or controlled by anything outside Himself. It is impossible for God to be God and not be sovereign.

As R. C. Sproul says,

> To say that God foreordains all that comes to pass is simply to say that God is sovereign over his entire creation. If something could come to pass apart from his sovereign permission, then that which came to pass would frustrate his sovereignty. If God refused to permit something to happen and it happened anyway, then whatever caused it to happen would have more authority and power than God himself. If there is any part of creation outside of God's sovereignty, then God is simply not sovereign. If God is not sovereign, then God is not God. If there is one single molecule in this universe running around loose, totally free of God's sovereignty, then we have no guarantee that a single promise of God will ever be fulfilled.... Sovereignty is not an issue peculiar to Calvinism, or even to Christianity. *Without sovereignty God cannot be God. If we reject divine sovereignty then we must embrace atheism* [emphasis mine].[33]

[32] Boettner, *Reformed Doctrine of Predestination*, 33.
[33] Sproul, R. C., *Chosen by God*, (Chicago, IL: Tyndale, 1986), 26–27.

Sovereignty is foundational to biblical understanding. God's plan re-lates to all things. Whatever is done in time was decreed by God before time began. This includes all things, great or small, light or darkness, pros-perity or disaster (James 1:17; Isaiah 45:7). Yet He is not the author of sin, even though He decreed it. The 1689 *London Baptist Confession of Faith* says it about as well as it can be said,

> From all eternity God decreed all that should happen in time, and this He did freely and unalterably, consulting only His own wise and holy will. Yet in so doing He does not become in any sense the author of sin, nor does He share responsibility for sin with sinners. Neither, by reason of His decree, is the will of any creature whom He has made violated; nor is the free working of second causes put aside; rather is it established. In all these matters the divine wisdom appears, as also does God's power and faithfulness in effecting that which He has purposed.[34]

There is a great deal of mystery in this. If God is good, why did He create a world in which evil could exist? Is He not almighty or is He not perfectly good? Was He somewhere else when Adam and Eve fell into sin? Did He not know that Lucifer the archangel would rebel and become the devil? Why didn't He simply kill the devil or at least wipe sin away when it first appeared? If God is in total control, why do men still defy and resist Him? One thing is certain, God is not the author of sin. Even more, nei-ther is He even capable of sin (James 1:13). Even though there is much we do not see, still God is always presented to us in Scripture as all powerful, perfectly holy, righteous and incapable of wrong or evil.

Yes, God did in some mysterious way decree all things that come to pass. Therefore, He must have ordained the fall of man and the entrance of sin into the world. If He did not allow sin's entrance, then it would not have happened. If it happened outside His will, then He is not sover-eign. We must conclude that God predetermined that sin should enter the world in just the way it did. That is the only consistent as well as biblical answer there is.

Amid all the mysteries, we can certainly affirm that His glory is dis-played in the exercise of His justice, against the backdrop of sin and evil.

---

[34] *A Faith to Confess: The Baptist Confession of Faith of 1689* (Liverpool, England: Carey Publications, 1975), 20. Supporting Scriptures: Numbers 23:19; Isaiah 46:10; John 19:11; Acts 4:27–28; Romans 9:15, 18; Ephesians 1:3–5, 11; Hebrews 6:17; James 1:13; 1 John 1:5.

On the other hand, His gracious love and mercy that He freely bestows on hell deserving sinners is displayed.

We must remember, God did not force it to happen. He created Adam and Eve upright and with free wills. They freely chose to sin (Ecclesiastes 7:29). God did not make them do it. He provided all kinds of deterrents to keep them from evil. They could have freely stayed away from the tree of the knowledge of good and evil and enjoyed all the other delights of living in the Garden of Eden. If Adam was created upright, had a free will unbound by sin, walking with God, and still disobeyed, who do we think we are to say we would have done better had we been there? We don't even come close to having the same privileges as he.

R. C. Sproul concludes:

> We must assume that God knew in advance that man would fall. We also must assume that he could have intervened to stop it. Or he could have chosen not to create us at all. We grant all those hypothetical possibilities. Bottom line, we know that he knew we would fall and that he went ahead and created us anyway. Why does that mean he is unloving? He also knew in advance that he was going to implement a plan of redemption for his fallen creation that would include a perfect manifestation of his justice and a perfect expression of his love and mercy. It was certainly loving of God to predestine the salvation of his people, those the Bible calls his "elect" or chosen ones.
>
> It is the non-elect that are the problem. If some people are not elected unto salvation then it would seem that God is not all that loving toward them. For them it seems that it would have been more loving of God not to have allowed them to be born.
>
> It is important to point out again that these problems arise for all Christians who believe in a sovereign God. These questions are not unique to a particular view of predestination. People argue that God is loving enough to provide a way of salvation for all sinners. Since Calvinism restricts salvation only to the elect, it seems to require a less loving God. On the surface at least, it seem that a non-Calvinist view provides an opportunity for vast numbers of people to be saved who would not be saved in the Calvinist view.... If the final decision for the salvation of fallen sinners were left in the hands of fallen sinners, we would despair of all hope that anyone would be saved.[35]

While these biblical teachings may seem deep and complicated, we can be sure they are all within God's hidden purpose. We do know that He

---

[35] Sproul, *Chosen by God*, 32–33.

has ordained to bring all sin into judgment and will never let it or Satan go beyond the limits He has fixed beforehand.

There are seemingly, from our standpoint, many things that work against His sovereignty. While the Bible does not answer all our questions, it does reveal with greatest clarity the wonderful nature and character of God. We are always assured that God is good. "For the Lord is good and his love endures forever; his faithfulness continues through all generations." (Psalm 100:5). Abraham said it thousands of years ago, "Will not the Judge of all the earth do right?" (Genesis 18:25). Also, He is almighty. These are the truths we must rest in and find our peace amid all our questions.

God has decreed sin for His own reasons and for His own glory. The greatest Christian thinkers or theologians cannot completely fathom this mystery. However, the Calvinistic system meets this and other problems head-on. To me, this is what is so thrilling. While readily acknowledging a lack of understanding in many things, the God-centered Calvinistic system, which emphasizes the sovereignty of God is, by far, the most logical, satisfying as well as the most scriptural position.

I gladly trust all the mysteries with Him who cannot be unfair or do anything wrong. Remember, they may be problems with us but not with God. They are simply a part of His eternal plan. If He wanted us to understand all mysteries, He would have told us. Our responsibility is to obey and rest in the truth of Deuteronomy 29:29, "The secret things belong to the Lord our God, but the things revealed belong to us and to our children forever, that we may follow all the words of this law."

God created man and placed him on earth. He fixed all the circumstances and details surrounding his existence from beginning to end (Acts 17:24–26). He not only established the laws that govern the universe but actually fixed their application. For example, the number of our days on earth are set beforehand (Psalm 139:16); the hairs on our heads are numbered and the small sparrow falls to the ground only when God wills it (Matthew 10:29–30).

Even though God does not violate human will, His sovereignty extends to the will. Pharaoh freely chose to rebel against God (Exodus 9:17) but God hardened his heart so that he would not let the Israelites go (Exodus 9:12). He is also able to melt the hearts of anyone He pleases, even the most obstinate and rebellious. Saul of Tarsus is a good example (Acts 9:3–10). There has probably never been a worse sinner on earth. He said it himself, "Christ Jesus came into the world to save sinners—of whom I am the worst" (1 Timothy1:15). If he saved Saul of Tarsus, why doesn't He reveal Himself in the same way to everyone? He could if He so pleased, because He is God. He has mercy on whom He wills (Romans 9:14, 16).

The big problem that most seem to have with this part of God's character is that they are deeply disturbed at the reality of being at the absolute disposal of God. Men by nature hate and resist this. They either become atheists, deny this part of His character, ignore Him altogether or bow to him and say, "My Lord and my God" (John 20:28). Jude spoke of this in his day, "In the very same way, these dreamers pollute their own bodies, reject authority and slander celestial beings" (Jude 8). People, in their depraved desire to be independent of God, speak evil of His kingly majesty and His power to do with His creatures what He pleases.

We like to speak of God's mercy, goodness and love and want to know that these are readily available to us. In much of the preaching today, the subject of His Lordship is conspicuously missing. Satan tried his best to destroy and replace God's sovereignty in the Garden of Eden (Genesis 3:1–5). Man did not gain a proper knowledge of good and evil. Instead, he became the slave to sin and died, just as God said he would (Genesis 2:17).

All Satan's children by nature resist the rule of God (Luke 19:14). C.H. Spurgeon said:

> If anything is hated bitterly, it is the out-and-out gospel of the grace of God, especially if that hateful word "sovereignty" is mentioned with it, Dare to say "He will have mercy on whom he will have mercy, and he will have compassion on whom he will have compassion" (Romans 9:15), and furious critics will revile you without stint. The modern religionist not only hates the doctrine of sovereign grace, but he raves and rages at the mention of it. He would sooner hear you blaspheme than preach election by the Father, atonement by the Son, or regeneration by the Spirit. If you want to see a man worked up till the Satanic is clearly uppermost, let some of the new divines hear you preach a free-grace sermon. A gospel which is after men will be welcomed by men; but, it needs a divine operation upon the heart and mind to make a man willing to receive into his inmost soul this distasteful gospel of the grace of God. My dear brethren, do not try to make it tasteful to carnal minds. Hide not the offence of the cross, lest you make it of none effect. The angles and corners of the gospel are its strength: to pare them off is to deprive it of power. Toning down is not the increase of strength, but the death of it. Why, even among the sects, you must have noticed that their distinguishing points are the horns of their power; and when these are practically omitted, the sect is effete. Learn, then, that if you take Christ out of Christianity, Christi-

anity is dead. If you move grace out of the gospel, the gospel is gone. If the people do not like the doctrine of grace, give them all the more of it. Whenever its enemies rail at a certain kind of gun, a wise military power will provide more of such artillery. A great General, going in before his king, stumbled over his own sword. "I see," said the king, "your sword is in the way." The warrior answered, "Your majesty's enemies have often felt the same." That our gospel offends the King's enemies is no regret to us.[36]

Spurgeon said again,

I preach the doctrines of grace because I see the holy result of them in believers. I confess they are none the less dear to me because the advanced school despises them; I should never think it a recommendation of a doctrine that it was new. Those truths which I preach to you is that of the Puritans: it is the doctrine of Calvin, the doctrine of Augustine, the doctrine of Paul, the doctrine of the Holy Ghost. The Author and Finisher of our faith himself taught this most blessed truth which well agreed with our text. (Ephesians 2:8). The doctrine of grace is the substance of the testimony of Jesus.[37]

The Sovereignty of God in His Decrees

God's decrees are an extension or outworking of His sovereignty. Because God is sovereign, He can and has decreed all things. J.P. Boyce gives the following definition, "The decrees of God may be defined as that just, wise, and holy purpose or plan by which eternally, and within himself, he determines all things whatsoever that come to pass."[38]

All that we see happening in our world is not taking place through luck, chance or accident. It may seem that way to us but it is really the mighty hand of God working all things in conformity with His own will (Ephesians 1:11). I detest anyone wishing me "good luck." I don't live by "luck", nor does anyone. The Bible tells us that God is even in charge of the dice that are thrown. "The lot is cast into the lap, but its every decision is from the Lord" (Proverbs 16:33). An interesting story took place in 1 Kings 22 that proves this point. We are told that King Ahab "took a

[36] C. H. Spurgeon, "Our Manifesto" (1891) in *The Metropolitan Tabernacle Pulpit*, vol. 37 (Pasadena, TX: Pilgrim Publications, 1980), 49.

[37] C. H. Spurgeon, excerpt from *The Sword and Trowel* (January 1887).

[38] Boyce, *Abstract of Systematic Theology*, 115.

chance" by going into battle. In verse 34, there was a soldier "who drew his bow at random" and shot an arrow. It struck Ahab and killed him; and dogs licked up his blood just as the Lord had prophesied (1 Kings 21:19–22). Most would say this happened only by chance. God prophesied it in order to accomplish His purpose of judgment.

A good way of illustrating God's decrees is by thinking of the building of a house, the making of a watch, the manufacturing of an automobile or ten thousand other things that require a predetermined plan. The wise builder and designer must prepare certain blueprints and specifications before anything can be done toward construction. While this is not a perfect illustration, the point is still clear. If people can be given credit for being this wise, can't we do the same for God? Yet, it is common to find those who seem to think that there are things God didn't know about, that took Him by surprise; things He didn't "bargain" for.

Man makes his plans but they are filled with error, sin and things he could not anticipate. According to many, God's plans are often hindered, frustrated, confused, reversed and even stopped. But the Scripture says, "I know that you can do all things; no plan of yours can be thwarted" (Job 42:2).

The following list of verses show some the characteristics of God's decrees.[39]

1. God's decrees are eternal:

That have been known for ages (Acts 15:18).

For he chose us in him before the creation of the world to be holy and blameless in his sight (Ephesians 1:4).

According to his eternal purpose which he accomplished in Christ Jesus our Lord (Ephesians 3:11).

He was chosen before the creation of the world, but was revealed in these last times for your sake (1 Peter 1:20).

But we ought always to thank God for you, brothers loved by the Lord, because from the beginning God chose you to be saved through

---

[39] This list is based on Boyce, *Abstract of Systematic Theology*, 124. See also Chapter 10: "The Decrees of God in General" in A. A. Hodge, *Outlines of Theology* (1879; reprint., Edinburgh: The Banner of Truth Trust, 1983), 200–213; and Charles Hodge, Systematic Theology (reprint, Grand Rapids, MI: Eerdmans, 1979), 533–549.

the sanctifying work of the Spirit and through belief in the truth
(2 Thessalonians 2:13).

Who has saved us and called us to a holy life—not because of anything we have done but because of his own purpose and grace. This
grace was given us in Christ Jesus before the beginning of time
(2 Timothy 1:9).

No, we speak of God's secret wisdom, a wisdom that has been hidden
and that God destined for our glory before time began (1 Corinthians
2:7).

2. God's decrees are changeless:

But the plans of the Lord stand firm forever, the purposes of his heart
through all generations (Psalm 33:11).

Remember the former things, those of long ago; I am God, and there
is no other; I am God, and there is none like me (Isaiah 46:9).

3. God's decrees comprehend all events:

At the end of that time, I, Nebuchadnezzar, raised my eyes toward
heaven, and my sanity was restored. Then I praised the Most High;
I honored and glorified him who lives forever. His dominion is an
eternal dominion; his kingdom endures from generation to generation. All the peoples of the earth are regarded as nothing. He does as
he pleases with the powers of heaven and the peoples of the earth.
No one can hold back his hand or say to him: "What have you done?"
(Daniel 4:34–35).

In him we were also chosen, having been predestined according to
the plan of him who works out everything in conformity with the
purpose of his will (Ephesians 1:11).

I make known the end from the beginning, from ancient times, what
is still to come. I say: My purpose will stand and I will do all that I
please (Isaiah 46:10).

Man's days are determined; you have decreed the number of his
months and have set limits he cannot exceed (Job 14:5).

The Lord works out everything for his own ends even the wicked for
a day of disaster (Proverbs 16:4).

He himself gives all men life and breath and everything else. From
one man he made every nation of men, that they should inhabit the

whole earth; and he determined the times set for them and the exact places where they should live (Acts 17:25–26).

All the days ordained for me were written in your book before one of them came to be (Psalm 139:16).

4. God's decrees comprehend the free actions of men:

For we are God's workmanship, created in Christ Jesus to do good works, which God prepared in advance for us to do. Therefore, remember that formerly you who are Gentiles by birth and called "uncircumcised" by those who call themselves "the circumcision" (that done in the body by the hands of men) (Ephesians 2:10–11).

For it is God who works in you to will and to act according to his good purpose (Philippians 2:13).

5. God's decrees comprehend the wicked actions of men:

This man was handed over to you by God's set purpose and foreknowledge; and you, with the help of wicked men, put him to death by nailing him to the cross (Acts 2:23).

Indeed Herod and Pontius Pilate met together with the Gentiles and the people of Israel in this city to conspire against your holy servant Jesus, whom you anointed. They did what your power and will had decided beforehand should happen (Acts 4:27–28).

When they had carried out all that was written about him, they took him down from the tree and laid him in a tomb (Acts 13:29).

And, "a stone that causes men to stumble and a rock that makes them fall." They stumble because they disobey the message— which is also what they were destined for (1 Peter 2:8).

For certain men whose condemnation was written about long ago have secretly slipped in among you. They are godless men, who change the grace of our God into a license for immorality and deny Jesus Christ our only Sovereign and Lord (Jude 4).

For God has put it into their hearts to accomplish his purpose by agreeing to give the beast their power to rule, until God's words are fulfilled (Revelation 17:17).

But God sent me ahead of you to preserve for you a remnant on earth and to save your lives by a great deliverance. 'So then, it was not you who sent me here, but God. He made me father to Pharaoh, lord of his entire household and ruler of all Egypt (Genesis 45:7–8).

You intended to harm me, but God intended it for good to accomplish what is now being done, the saving of many lives (Genesis 50:20).

Rise up, O Lord, confront them, bring them down; rescue me from the wicked by your sword. O Lord, by your hand save me from such men, from men of this world whose reward is in this life (Psalm 17:13–14).

Woe to the Assyrian, the rod of my anger, in whose hand is the club of my wrath! (Isaiah 10:5).

6. God's decrees are not conditional:

Many are the plans in a man's heart, but it is the Lord's purposes that prevails (Proverbs 19:21).

The Lord Almighty has sworn, Surely, as I have planned, so it will be, and as I have purposed, so it will stand. For the Lord Almighty has purposed, and who can thwart him? His hand is stretched out, and who can turn it back? (Isaiah 14:24, 27).

Yet, before the twins were born or had done anything good or bad— in order that God's purpose in election might stand: not by works but by him who calls (Romans 9:11–12).

7. God's decrees are sovereign:

Who has understood the mind of the Lord, or instructed him as his counselor? Whom did the Lord consult to enlighten him, and who taught him the right way? (Isaiah 40:13–14).

All the peoples of the earth are regarded as nothing. He does as he pleases with the powers of heaven and the peoples of the earth. No one can hold back his hand or say to him: "What have you done?" (Daniel 4:35).

At that time Jesus said, "I praise you, Father, Lord of heaven and earth, because you have hidden these things from the wise and learned, and revealed them to little children. Yes, Father, for this was your good pleasure" (Matthew 11: 25–26).

Yet, before the twins were born or had done anything good or bad— in order that God's purpose in election might stand: For he says to Moses, "I will have mercy on whom I have mercy, and I will have compassion on whom I have compassion." It does not, therefore, depend on man's desire or effort, but on God's mercy. For the Scripture says to Pharaoh: "I raised you up for this very purpose, that I might display my power in you and that my name might be proclaimed in all the earth." Therefore God has mercy on whom he wants to have mercy, and He hardens whom He wants to harden (Romans 9:11, 15–18).

...He predestined us to be adopted as His sons through Jesus Christ, in accordance with His pleasure and will... In Him we were also chosen, having been predestined according to the plan of Him who works out everything in conformity with the purpose of His will... (Ephesians 1: 5, 11).

8. God's decrees include the means:

But we ought always to thank God for you, brothers loved by the Lord, because from the beginning God chose you to be saved through the sanctifying work of the Spirit and through belief in the truth (2 Thessalonians 2:13).

...who have been chosen according to the foreknowledge of God the Father, through the sanctifying work of the Spirit, for obedience to Jesus Christ and sprinkling by his blood: Grace and peace be yours in abundance (1 Peter 1:2).

9. God's decrees comprehend the free actions of men:

Indeed Herod and Pontius Pilate met together with the Gentiles and the people of Israel in this city to conspire against your holy servant Jesus, whom you anointed. They did what your power and will had decided beforehand should happen (Acts 4: 27, 28).

For we are God's workmanship, created in Christ Jesus to do good works, which God prepared in advance for us to do (Ephesians 2:10).

10. God grants to His people the faith and obedience required for salvation:

For it is by grace you have been saved, through faith—and this not from yourselves, it is the gift of God (Ephesians 2:8).

...for it is God who works in you to will and to act according to his good purpose (Philippians 2:13).

Those who oppose him he must gently instruct, in the hope that God will grant them repentance leading them to a knowledge of the truth... (2 Timothy 2:25).

11. God's decrees renders the event certain:

From that time on Jesus began to explain to his disciples that he must go to Jerusalem and suffer many things at the hands of the elders, chief priests and teachers of the law, and that he must be killed and on the third day be raised to life (Matthew 16: 21).

Jesus took the Twelve aside and told them, "We are going up to Jerusalem, and everything that is written by the prophets about the Son of Man will be fulfilled. He will be handed over to the Gentiles. They will mock him, insult him, spit on him, flog him and kill him. On the third day he will rise again." He told them, "This is what is written: The Christ will suffer and rise from the dead on the third day..." (Luke 18:31–33; 24:46).

This man was handed over to you by God's set purpose and foreknowledge; and you, with the help of wicked men, put him to death by nailing him to the cross....When they had carried out all that was written about him, they took him down from the tree and laid him in a tomb (Acts 2:23; 13:29).

No doubt there have to be differences among you to show which of you have God's approval (1 Corinthians 11:19).

12. Even though God decreed the free actions of men, men are non-the-less responsible:

This man was handed over to you by God's set purpose and foreknowledge; and you, with the help of wicked men, put him to death by nailing him to the cross. But this is how God fulfilled what he had foretold through all the prophets, saying that his Christ would suffer. Indeed Herod and Pontius Pilate met together with the Gentiles and the people of Israel in this city to conspire against your holy servant Jesus, whom you anointed. They did what your power and will had decided beforehand should happen (Acts 2:23, 3:18; 4:27, 28).

13. God has decreed all things that come to pass, even evil and disaster, for His own glory and sovereign purpose:

I am the Lord, and there is no other; apart from me there is no God. I will strengthen you, though you have not acknowledged me, so that form the rising of the sun to the place of its setting men may know there is none besides me. I am the Lord, and there is no other. I form the light and create darkness, I bring prosperity and create disaster;

I, the Lord, do all these things. "You heavens above, rain down righteousness; let the clouds shower it down. Let the earth open wide, let salvation spring up, let righteousness grow with it; I, the Lord, have created it. Woe to him who quarrels with his Maker, to him who is but a potsherd among the potsherds on the ground. Does the clay say to the potter, 'What are you making?' Does your work say, 'He has no hands?' Woe to him who says to his father, 'What have you begotten?' or to his mother, 'What have you brought to birth?'"(Isaiah 45:5-10).

See now that I myself am He! There is no god besides me. I put to death and I bring to life, I have wounded and I will heal, and no one can deliver out of my hand (Deuteronomy 32:39).

The LORD said to him, "Who gave man his mouth? Who makes him deaf or mute? Who gives him sight or makes him blind? Is it not I, the LORD? (Exodus 4:11).

He called down famine on the land and destroyed all their supplies of food (Psalm 105:16).

When they first lived there, they did not worship the LORD; so he sent lions among them and they killed some of the people (2 Kings 17:25).

Who can speak and have it happen if the Lord has not decreed it? Is it not from the mouth of the Most High that both calamities and good things come? (Lamentations 3:37-38).

The LORD works out everything for his own ends— even the wicked for a day of disaster (Proverbs 16:4).

You are not a God who takes pleasure in evil; with you the wicked cannot dwell (Psalm 5:4).

It does not, therefore, depend on man's desire or effort, but on God's mercy. For the Scripture says to Pharoah: "I raised you up for this very purpose, that I might display my power in you and that my name might be proclaimed in all the earth." Therefore God has mercy on whom he wants to have mercy, and he hardens whom he wants to harden. One of you will say to me: "Then why does God still blame us? For who resists his will?" But who are you, O man, to talk back to God? "Shall what is formed say to him who formed it, 'Why did you make me like this?'" Does not the potter have the right to make out of the same lump of clay some pottery for noble purposes and some for common use? (Romans 9:16-21).

In his commentary on the *Westminster Confession of Faith*, G. I. Williamson says,

> The free actions of men are also predestined by God. Please note: these acts are both free and predestined. That is, those who commit these acts do so because they want to. And yet those acts which they do are predetermined by God so that Scripture says they must happen. Christ said, "it must needs be that offenses come: but woe to that man by whom the offense cometh." This statement recognizes two things: (1) the certainty of the occurrence of a future event, and (2) that those who will perform the act will do so freely and therefore with guilt. So in Acts 2:23 we read of Christ "being delivered by the determinate counsel and foreknowledge of God," and yet also as "taken, and by wicked hands crucified and slain." "Of a truth...against...Jesus...both Herod, and Pontius Pilate, with the Gentiles and the people of Israel, were gathered together, for to do whatsoever (God's) hand and counsel determined to be done" (Acts 4:27, 28). As God predetermines evil actions which are freely performed, so he predetermines good actions which are also freely performed. Christians repent, believe and seek to do the will of God because they want to. But in this case "it is God which worketh in (them) to will and to do of his good pleasure" (Philippians 2:13). There is, in this case, an internal operation of God's Spirit, which is wholly absent from the wicked. But this still does not mean that the good (converted) any more than the wicked (unconverted) are not free in doing what God has predestined that they shall do.[40]

The wisest, best, and most beneficial thing anyone can do is to stop resisting God's sovereignty and yield to Him in humble submission. There is nothing more blessed. Foolish indeed is the individual who runs from God. Wise indeed is he who runs to God and worships Him in all His glory. God is God. No one will ever comprehend Him completely. He cannot be put into our little boxes of human reasoning. "As the heavens are higher than the earth, so are my ways higher than your ways and my thoughts than your thoughts" (Isaiah 55:9).I trust the doxology that the Apostle Paul gave in Romans 11:33–36 will be ours as we meditate on this immense truth:

---

[40] G. I. Williamson, *The Westminster Confession of Faith for Study Classes* (Phillipsburg, NJ: Presbyterian and Reformed Publishing, 1964), 30-31.

Oh, the depth of the riches of the wisdom and knowledge of God! How unsearchable his judgments and his paths beyond tracing out! "Who has known the mind of the Lord? Or who has been his counselor?" "Who has ever given to God, that God should repay him?" For from him and through him and to him are all things. To him be the glory forever! Amen

5

The Will of God

In order to guard against a great deal of confusion, it is essential to have a clear understanding of what the Bible teaches about the will of God. There have been some popular yet inadequate distinctions applied to it that do not correctly define it. Some, for example, have spoken in terms of the "permissive" will of God. But simply to say that God has given His permission might suggest that there are things in existence that somehow overpowered God or "sneaked in" without His knowledge. This idea takes away from His sovereignty. The following, I believe, is a more biblically accurate way to understand God's will.

The Secret or Decretive Will of God

This aspect of God's will cannot be thwarted nor can it be completely understood. It includes all that comes to pass, even Satan and sin. In this designation, all things are in His will whether we recognize it or not. God's will is unchangeable and will come to pass with or without man's coopera- tion or obedience. Even the smallest detail will be accomplished. It is ir- resistible and cannot fail. Nothing stands in its way that can hinder or slow it down. It has the future and God's ultimate purpose primarily in view.

God's decreed will can only be made known if, and only if He chooses to make it so. It is mysterious but we can always know that God knows exactly what He's doing. He has a flawless plan that He is carefully work- ing out that will be to His eternal glory. To know that our God is in charge of all things is the most blessed reality there is. This truth provides for us God's deepest and most meaningful peace.

Consider the following verses and passages Scriptures that verify the decretive will of God:

1. In Creation and Providence

> The Lord does whatever pleases him, in the heavens and on the earth in the seas and all their depths (Psalm 135:6).

> "O house of Israel, can I not do with you as this potter does?" declares the Lord. "Like clay in the hand of the potter, so are you in my hand, O house of Israel" (Jeremiah 18:6).

> You are worthy, our Lord and God, to receive glory and honor and power, for you created all things, and by your will they were created and have their being (Revelation 4:11).

2. In Human Government

> The king's heart is in the hand of the Lord; he directs it like a watercourse wherever he pleases (Proverbs 21:1).

> All the peoples of the earth are regarded as nothing. He does as he pleases with the powers of heaven and the peoples of the earth. No one can hold back his hand or say to him: "What have you done?" (Daniel 4:35).

3. In Christ's Death on the Cross

> Father, if you are willing, take this cup from me; yet not my will, but yours be done (Luke 22:42).

> This man was handed over to you by God's set purpose and foreknowledge; and you, with the help of wicked men, put him to death by nailing him to the cross (Acts 2:23).

4. In God's Electing Love

> What then shall we say? Is God unjust? Not at all! For he says to Moses, "I will have mercy on whom I have mercy, and I will have compassion on whom I have compassion." It does not, therefore, depend on man's desire or effort, but on God's mercy (Romans 9:14–16).

> In him we were also chosen, having been predestined according to the plan of him who works out everything in conformity with the purpose of his will (Ephesians 1:11).

5. In the Regeneration of Believers

> He chose to give us birth through the Word of truth, that we might be a kind of firstfruits of all he created (James 1:18).

6. In the Santification of Believers

> For it is God who works in you to will and to act according to his good purpose (Philippians 2:13).

7. In the Suffering of Believers

> It is better, if it is God's will, to suffer for doing good than for doing evil (1 Peter 3:17).

> For it has been granted to you on behalf of Christ not only to believe on him, but also to suffer for him (Philippians 1:29).

The Preceptive or Revealed Will of God

Some call it His will of command. This is made known in His Word. It is that which we are to follow. Over and over God's will is revealed to us. It pertains to our duty, works, service and commitment. It is here that I find God's commands for me which I am to meticulously obey all the days of my life. It is not optional or just good advise.

Herein is defined what is right and wrong. This part of God's will can be thwarted, hindered and even stopped. By not obeying God's precepts I can and do incur the chastening of God. By my sins of commission or omission I grieve the Holy Spirit (Ephesians 4:30). God's revealed will is never done perfectly, even by the greatest of God's people.

The lost sinner's corruption in sin will not let him acceptably accomplish God's revealed will, even though, from our view, he may do many commendable things. All our righteous acts are as filthy rags in God's sight (Isaiah 64:6). It is only by the justifying blood of Christ that our works are made acceptable, and then only through pure motives and Holy Spirit energy (1 John 1:7; 1 Corinthians 3:12–15).

Additional clarity comes when we understand that God's decreed will is accomplished even in the breaking of His preceptive will. In the worse kind of satanic activity and human disobedience God's original decreed and eternal purpose is perfectly done. The wise counsel and mighty power of God is never hindered or stopped even when evil events occur and wicked people have their way (Acts 2:23; Genesis 50:20). In doing so God always acts consistent with and never in violation of the free agency of man.

The following are some texts that speak of God's revealed will.

> Not everyone who says to me, "Lord, Lord," will enter the kingdom of heaven, but only he who does the will of my Father who is in heaven (Matthew 7:21).

> For whoever does the will of my Father in heaven is my brother and sister and mother (Matthew 12:50).

> My food is to do the will of him who sent me and to finish his work (John 4:34).

> If anyone chooses to do God's will, he will find out whether my teaching comes from God or whether I speak on my own (John 7:17).

> Do not conform any longer to the pattern of this world, but be transformed by the renewing of your mind. Then you will be able to test and approve what God's will is—his good, pleasing and perfect will (Romans 12:2).

The Dispositional Will of God

It is helpful to understand this aspect of God's will because it gives us insight into such Scriptures as Ezekiel 18:23, 32 and 33:11.

> Do I take any pleasure in the death of the wicked?… Am I not pleased when they turn from their ways and live. For I take no pleasure in the death of anyone…but rather that they turn from their ways and live.

Consider also 2 Peter 3:9.

> He is patient with you not wanting anyone to perish, but everyone to come to repentance (2 Peter 3:9).

I will deal with 2 Peter 3:9 in more detail in another chapter. Here I simply want to show how the dispositional will of God applies. It means that God does not delight or take joy in pouring out His just and well deserved judgment on guilty sinners. It is much the same as a loving, caring judge who must see that justice is carried out. He is right in condemning and sentencing criminals. Injustice is committed if he doesn't. He knows that he must because it is right. However, there is a sense of sorrow in which he takes no pleasure at all.

God is just and will not wink at sin. He will not be mocked. However, there is a sense in which He is grieved. Jesus was sorrowful when He looked over the city of Jerusalem and said,

> O Jerusalem, Jerusalem, you who kill the prophets and stone those sent to you, how often I have longed to gather your children together, as a hen gathers her chicks under her wings, but you were not willing (Luke 13:34).

Judgment came but He was sorrowful and actually wept. God does not delight in sentencing law-breakers to their just condemnation as guilty children of Adam (Micah 7:18–19).

Confusion is often experienced when we read such passages as, "And he (Jesus) did not do many miracles there because of their lack of faith," (Matthew 13:58). "Again and again they put God to the test; they vexed (KJV uses the word, "limited") the Holy One of Israel," (Psalm 78:41). "You always resist the Holy Spirit!" (Acts 7:51). These simply represent ways in which His commands, laws and precepts can be and are disobeyed. His decreed will cannot be limited or frustrated by anyone or anything, but His preceptive will is either partially or completely disobeyed by all. Only Christians can acceptably keep God's commands and that only imperfectly at best.

Many people think this presents an unsolvable and unworkable problem. It seems that God has two wills that oppose each other. However, with some careful thought, we come to see the harmony of these two designations of God's will rather than a contradiction.

First of all, God cannot contradict or be inconsistent with Himself. Although, from our limited view, this seems unworkable; from God's view it is not. All God's works are good, perfect, glorious and with eternal purpose. Just because we don't understand, it does not mean God doesn't. Let's not sin against the Almighty by trying to bring Him down to our level. We must remember that our reason is not only limited but corrupted with sin. For this reason alone, if for nothing else, we should know that God, who is perfectly wise, righteous, just, loving and all-powerful will only and always do what is right.

Second, as we have already seen, God's sovereignty is violated if anything is outside His control. Either He is in control or He is not. To say there is anything in existence that inadvertently crept in without God knowing is to take away from His omnipotence and omniscience. All things have to be His will because of who He is. If God be God, how can it be any other way?

The prevailing belief in the Christian world is that God has chosen to limit Himself to man's will. The idea goes like this: God made man in His own image and gave him freedom of choice. He is the master of his fate and captain of his soul. God exerts all sorts of good influences upon man but will not violate man's power to decide for himself. Hence, He stands by waiting to see what man will do and He acts in response to man's choices.

Careful examination will remind us that man is dead in trespasses and sins and his choices are not pleasing to God. The very idea that the sovereign God doesn't act until sinful, wicked, self-centered man does is nothing short of blasphemous. This would completely dethrone God. If God limits Himself to man's decisions, He would never accomplish anything.

Our response to God's decretive will should be complete trust; to His preceptive will explicit obedience. With regard to His dispositional we should share His heart.

6

The Foreknowledge of God

It is with the doctrine of foreknowledge that many think they can forever hush the Calvinist. Almost always the argument is brought forward as follows: God knows and sees all things. He is well aware of everything before it ever happens. Because of this He knows all to whom the gospel will be preached and all who will believe. It is, therefore, upon this basis that He elects people whom He sees in His foreknowledge will freely choose to be saved. He chooses those who will choose Him. It is with this view that people try to "protect" God and man's "free will" at once. While this seems to solve all the problems connected with it, actually it leaves us with greater problems. In reality, the biblical doctrine of foreknowledge is one of the most powerful proofs of God's sovereignty in salvation.

To begin with, foreknowledge means far more than mere objective knowledge of future events. Dr. Millard Erickson, in his book *Introducing Christian Doctrine*, gives us a more biblical explanation:

> "...the Arminian argument that God's foreordaining is based upon his foreknowledge is not persuasive. For the Hebrew word "yada", which seems to lie behind the references to "foreknowledge" in Romans 8:29 and I Peter 1:1-2 (NIV), signifies more than an advance knowledge or precognition. It carries the connotation of a very positive and intimate relationship. It suggests looking with favor upon or loving someone, and is even used of sexual relations. What is in view, then, is not a neutral advance knowledge of what someone will do, but an affirmative choice of that person. Against this Hebraic background it appears likely that the references to foreknowledge in Romans and I Peter are presenting

foreknowledge not as the grounds for predestination, but as a confirmation of it."[41]

Take particular note of the following various translations of Romans 8:29, where the word *foreknowledge* is used:

- " For those whom he had marked out from the first he predestined to be made like his Son" (*An American Translation*, Smith and Goodspeed; Chicago: Uinversity of Chicago Press, 1912).

- "For whom He fore-approved He also fore-appointed to be conformed unto the image of His Son" (*The Emphasized Bible*, Joseph B. Rotherham; Grand Rapids: Kregel, 1959).

- "For those whom God had already chosen he had also set apart to become like his Son" (*Good News for Modern Man*, London: British and Foreign Bible Society, 1966).

- "For he previously knew them, and appointed them to conformity with the image of his Son" (*The Holy Bible in Modern English*, Ferrar Fenton: London; Black, 1903).

- "They are the ones he chose specially long ago and intended to become true images of his Son" (*The Jerusalem Bible*, ed. Alexander Jones; New York: Doubleday & Co., 1966).

- " For God knew his own before ever they were, and also ordained that they should be shaped to the likeness of his Son" (*The New English Bible* (Oxford University Press and Cambridge, 1970).

- "For long ago, before they ever came into being, God both knew them and marked them out to become like the pattern of his Son" (*The New Testament: A New Translation*, Vol. 2 (William Barclay; London: Collins, 1969).

- " For he decreed of old that those whom he predestined should share the likeness of his Son" (*The New Testament: A New Translation* (James Moffatt; New York: Hodder & Stroughton, no date).

[41] Millard J. Erickson, *Introducing Christian Doctrine* (Grand Rapids, MI, Baker Academic,1992, 2001), 303.

- "Because those whom He foreordained He also marked out be-forehand as those who were to be conformed to the derived image of His Son" (*The New Testament: An Expanded Translation* (Kenneth S. West; Grand Rapids: Eerdmans, 1961).

- "For those on whom He set His heart beforehand He marked off as His own to make like His Son" (*The New Testament: A Translation in the Language of the People* (Charles B. Williams; Chicago: Moody Press, 1937; Footnoted: "Literally, foreknew, but in the LXX used as translated.)

- "For those whom God chose from the first he also did predestinate to be conformed to the image of his Son" (*The Twentieth Century New Testament* (Chicago: Moody Bible Institute, 1967).

- "For those whom He foreknew – of whom He was aware and loved beforehand – He also destined from the beginning (foreordaining them) to be molded into the image of His Son [and share inwardly His likeness], that He might become the first-born among many brethren" (*The Amplified Bible* (Grand Rapids, Zondervan Publishing House, 1964).

Let's examine the Apostle Peter's uses of the term foreknowledge. First, in his sermon at Pentecost he said, "This man was handed over to you by God's set purpose and foreknowledge, and you, with the help of wicked men, put him to death by nailing him to the cross" (Acts 2:23). Here, it is made very clear that God's purpose in the crucifixion was eternal in nature. Jesus was "the Lamb that was slain from the creation of world" (Revelation 13:8). This does not mean that God saw the cross in the future but couldn't do anything about it. God did not, out of desperation, simply try to make the best of the situation. Not at all! Salvation was "promised before the beginning of time" (Titus 1:1–2). God decreed the crucifixion. It was predestined. To Peter, "foreknowledge" is plainly seen to be God's deliberate choice and foreordained purpose.

It is interesting to note here that "wicked men" crucified Christ. While finite man cannot totally understand the sovereignty of God and the responsibility of man, both are still undeniable facts. This text gives us much light on the subject. These "wicked men" were still regarded as wicked, even though they were unwittingly, fulfilling God's eternal plan. They were still responsible for their actions and would be held accountable. Men freely choose to sin and live in rebellion against God, yet, at the same time, God perfectly fulfills His eternal purpose through it all. This is a clear example in seeing that God is not the author of sin.

The Devil is the author and creator of sin and we, his children, always want to carry out his desires (John 8:44). God certainly does not make us sin. "When tempted, no one should say, 'God is tempting me.' For God cannot be tempted by evil, nor does he tempt anyone; but each one is tempted when, by his own evil desire, he is dragged away and enticed" (James 1:13–14).

Exactly how God perfectly, righteously, justly and infallibly accomplishes His eternal plan, even through the worst kind of wickedness, is far beyond our capacity to understand. Yet, it is all the more reason to exalt and praise His mighty Name.

Peter again uses "foreknowledge" in his first epistle. The Greek word is *prognosis* (1:2) and a different form of the same word is used in the same chapter in verse 20. Verse 2 says, "who have been chosen according to the foreknowledge of God the Father." This seems to be clear proof of conditional election; that God looked down through the ages and saw those "worthy ones," who, because of their faith or merit or both, would choose Him. This makes man sovereign and God powerless until man's choice is made. It puts God in the very precarious position of always being uncertain as to what He's going to do. He has to check with man before He acts. That's not the God of the Bible! It also takes away entirely from the doctrine of election itself. The very point Peter is making is that God is sovereign and that He chooses. Again I say, if God waited on sinful man to choose Him first, He would wait forever because man will not come (John 5:40).

In verse 20 the text says, "He (Christ) was chosen (same root word used in verse 2 for foreknowledge) before the creation of the world, but was revealed in these last times for your sake." By no means can this refer to God's mere knowledge of what Christ would do. It is very clear in the text that God had intimate knowledge of Christ and deliberately elected Him before the creation of the world. Christ was "a chosen and precious cornerstone" (1 Peter 2:6). It also becomes clear in verse 2 that God had intimate knowledge of and deliberately chose His elect ones in eternity in the same way He knew Christ. Thus we have yet another strong case in favor of sovereign grace.

There are similar accounts in Scripture of God's intimate knowledge and deliberate choice of others. Jeremiah learned this from God about himself, "Before I formed you in the womb I knew you, before you were born I set you apart; I appointed you as a prophet to the nations" (Jeremiah 1:5). Also, in Exodus 33:17, the Lord said to Moses, "I will do the very thing you have asked, because I am pleased with you and I know you by name." Again in Amos 3:2, He said to Israel "You only have I chosen (KJV uses "known") of all families of the earth." This same idea is used in Genesis 4:1 in speaking of Adam's intimate relationship with Eve.

In John 10:4, 14,15,27, Jesus speaks of His intimate knowledge of and love for His sheep. The same idea is conveyed in Matthew 7:23, in which Jesus said, "I never knew you. Away from me, you evildoers." Jesus was certainly not saying He never had a knowledge of those who would be damned. Rather, He speaks of a vital, personal, loving relationship. In other words, foreknowledge equals forelove or those whom God set His love upon before creation.

One of the most convincing truths about foreknowledge in favor of sovereign grace is found in the very nature of its meaning. To foreknow is to prefix or predetermine. For those who insist on arguing in favor of conditional election, the following question must be answered: How can anything foreknown not be predetermined? The very fact that something is foreknown is as good as saying that it will most surely happen. Foreknowledge and foreordination are like two sides to the same coin. Future events, whatever they may be, if known by God, must, of necessity be fixed. Actually, with God, it is not foreknowledge. The "fore" is more to accommodate our limited view in time. It is complete knowledge or omniscience. God does not live in the realm of time. He knows and sees all things at once; past, present and future.

Something else of interest relative to foreknowledge is to study biblical prophecy. The word itself means "to tell forth." Many times that "telling forth" pertains to future events. This is proof in itself of predestination. It is inconsistent, as well as unbiblical, to believe in God's ability to foretell future events and at the same time deny predestination. Foreknown future events must of necessity be prefixed. Arminians are often those who preach the loudest about God's revelations of the future. They need to know that they are unwittingly also preaching predestination.

Calvinists are sometimes accused of believing in a "monster God" who capriciously decrees to create people, to elect some for eternal life and others for eternal damnation without letting them have a say so in the matter. Those accusers do not seem to realize that their view of foreknowledge exposes enormous error. In other words, God foresaw that some would be lost. Why would He create them if He knew they would be forever lost in hell? After all, He is God isn't He? No one forced Him to do it. If He is trying to save everyone (this is the Arminian claim), couldn't He at least have created only those whom He knew would receive Christ? Does He work against Himself? Can He not make up His mind? Is He unsure of His own purposes? Can it be possible that He acted foolishly? He gave man the ability to choose to believe, yet knew before creation, that untold millions would never even hear the gospel, much less believe? It looks like He could have at least made sure each person would hear the way to be saved. Yet throughout history we all know that millions have never even heard the name of Jesus, much less heard a clear presentation of the gospel.

Besides all this, when this view of foreknowledge is believed, it takes all the meaning out of the doctrine itself. What sense would there be in God foreknowing and electing those whom He knows would elect themselves?

If the Arminian is truely honest and consistent, he must admit that he actually denies foreknowledge altogether. He is really saying that his God is either capricious, unjust and merciless or finite, ignorant and limited in knowledge, power and wisdom, or both. In all honesty, he really must admit that this is not God at all.

I much prefer to believe in God as He has revealed Himself in the Bible. He, in sovereign and unfathomable love and wisdom, chose an unnumbered multitude out of Adam's sinful race to mercifully and infallibly save. He then righteously and justly allowed condemnation to remain upon the rest of fallen humanity. In doing so, He is glorified in showing mercy toward those who do not deserve it and in justice toward those who do deserve it. The God of the Bible is infinitely loving, unspeakably gracious and powerful to save. Admittedly, there remains many mysteries. The greatest theological minds have never been able to solve them. However, the Calvinistic system does not compromise the Bible in an effort to make it all fit into man's limited understanding. The Arminian should realize the enormous problems in his system before he points an accusing finger at the Calvinist.

7

The Grace of God

Exactly what is grace? We talk much about it. We sing about it even more. Perhaps the most famous and widely known gospel hymn is "Amazing Grace." All true Christians agree that salvation is by grace alone. To deny this is to deny the faith.

It is interesting that even cults and other religions talk about grace. However, precisely how grace is understood in salvation is the point of controversy that has raged since biblical days. To have a thorough understanding of it is of utmost importance. If we are not clear at this point, then we will inevitably go astray. Our presuppositions about grace must be correct.

The most common New Testament word for grace is *charis*, which means,

> to rejoice…joy, favor…a kindness granted or desired, a benefit, thanks, gratitude….A favor done without expectation of return; absolute freeness of the loving kindness of God to men finding its only motive in the bounty and freeheartedness of the Giver; unearned and unmerited favor…grace affects man's sinfulness and not only forgives the repentant sinner, but brings joy and thankfulness to him.[42]

The definition I most prefer is, "God's unmerited loving kindness and tender mercy freely bestowed upon guilty, undeserving sinners." *Baker's Dictionary of Theology* says this,

---

[42] Spiros Zodhiates, ed. *The Key Hebrew-Greek Study Bible* (Iowa Falls, IA: World Bible Publishers, 1988), 1739; entry #5485.

It is quite clear that the NT overwhelmingly associates the word grace
with Christ, either directly ("the grace of our Lord Jesus Christ"), or else
by implication as the executor of the grace of God. It does this…because
it is in his incarnate Son that God puts into effect his being for us, shows
us that he is for us and reconciles us to himself, bringing us over to his
side, to be for him. Since all this comes to pass only by the incarnate
activity of Christ, we may say that grace means Jesus Christ, and Jesus
Christ means grace. He is the grace of God toward us. [43]

This grace is costly and precious because it is the very basis of our redemption in Christ. There is no degree of credit that man deserves. There
is no basis for human boasting. The gospel of free grace is the only true
gospel. It has to be of grace, else man could never have an interest in it.
That's why it is a gift.

> All who believe…are justified freely by his grace through the redemp-
> tion that came by Christ Jesus (Romans 3:22, 24).

> Now when a man works, his wages are not credited to him as a gift,
> but as an obligation. However, to the man who does not work but
> trusts God who justifies the wicked, his faith is credited as righteous-
> ness (Romans 4:4–5).

> And if by grace, then it is no longer by works; if it were, grace would
> no longer be grace (Romans 11:6).

Throughout church history, there have been basically three views of
grace relative to salvation:

(1) It has been taught that salvation is not by grace, yet the term "grace
of God" is used. Sound silly? Yes! Is it heretical? Most definitely! Yet it has
been around in varying forms for centuries. It is the belief that man has the
innate ability to save himself through moral, religious and ethical behavior.
In early church history, a British monk named Pelagius tried to teach that
Christianity was comprised of pagan morality. He was condemned as a
heretic at the Council of Ephesus in 431 AD and his system of doctrine
was labeled "Pelagianism." He taught that Christ's work on the cross was
not necessary. The term "grace of God" was used but only in reference to
the "noble creature" who could actually earn the right to go to heaven.

[43] E. F. Harrison, G. W. Bromiley and C. F. H. Henry, eds., *Baker's Dictionary of Theology* (Grand Rapids, MI: Baker, 1960), 257–258.

(2) Others have taught that salvation is mostly of grace but not completely. There are all kinds of systems that teach this. It is best represented in Arminianism or what has been called semi-Pelagianism. The central idea is that Christ has made salvation possible but there is still something man must do. It is a mixture of works and grace. Some systems emphasize more grace and some more works. Either way, it is faulty.

This mixture of grace and works is what Paul had to deal with in the Galatian heresy. Also, this was a very strategic and momentous issue with the New Testament Church in Acts 15 at the Council of Jerusalem. There, after much controversy, it was stated emphatically, "We believe it is through the grace of our Lord Jesus that we are saved" (Acts 15:11).

Mixing works with grace has been a menace to pure grace throughout Christian history. The idea is that God has done His part, now it's left up to man. God is said to play the major role, but it is the human contribution that makes it complete. It can be a number of things such as, cooperation with the Holy Spirit, decisionism, moral and ethical works, obedience, perseverance, baptism, church membership, etc.

At times I've heard preachers say, including myself, "God has done all He can. Now the rest is up to you." This presents a "poor God" image that dishonors the sovereign God who does as He pleases (Daniel 4:35), has mercy on whom He wills (Romans 9:15) and is able to save to the uttermost (Hebrews 7:25). In this system, if logically followed, you can get out as easily as you can get in. Since man has to do something to complete the process in order to get in, he can also do something to terminate it. As he chooses Christ for salvation, he can also reject Him and be lost again.

There is a more moderate form of Arminianism that much of the Christian world believes (most Southern Baptists fit into this category), which strongly embraces the doctrine of eternal security. However, the stricter Arminian, who believes you can lose salvation, is more consistent and logical by believing that it is possible to fall from grace.

(3) The biblical position is that salvation is entirely by grace. That is why it is called "sovereign grace" because it is only and always by God's mercy. The cross is absolutely necessary and totally sufficient for the salvation of sinners. There is no room whatsoever for any kind of human boasting. When true grace is realized, there is not a feeling of exclusivism or "better-than-thou." A recipient of this grace understands that he is only a sinner, deserving of hell, but saved by grace. Jerom Zanchius says,

> The greatest saint cannot triumph over the most abandoned sinner, but is
> led to refer the entire praise of his salvation, both from sin and hell, to the

mere goodwill and sovereign purpose of God, who hath graciously made him to differ from that world which lieth in wickedness.[44]

All the saved person can say when he views the worst lost sinner is, "There go I but for the grace of God." All the credit and glory goes to Jesus Christ. We don't even have the ability to come to Christ, repent or believe. The will is bound by sin and only God can free that stubborn will in the day of His power (Psalm 110:3; Romans 9:16; John 1:13: Philippians 2:13). We can't "decide" for Christ until the Spirit draws us (John 6:44). No man can repent on his own. This is a grace gift (Acts 5:31, 11:18) along with saving faith (Ephesians 2:8; Philippians 1:29). People do not come to Christ because of their natural goodness or wisdom or superior religious training. Nor should anyone ever pretend that they are a little better or more intelligent than others because they have received Christ. Our attitudes should always be that of Paul when he said, "I am what I am by the grace of God" (1 Corinthians 15:10).

At the cross Christ purchased our redemption and delivered us from sin and unbelief. Christ Jesus came into the world to save sinners and only sinners (Matthew 9:13). He didn't come simply to make salvation possible. He is actually accomplishing salvation and will not stop until all His sheep come into the fold (John 10:11, 14–16, 27–29).

The question sometimes arises, "Does God treat everyone the same and give equal opportunity for all to be saved?" In the light of man's condemned state before God, the answer is "no." We are treated as condemned criminals before a holy God. Many have the mistaken idea that God owes us something. As sinful rebels, God owes us nothing. We deserve nothing but hell. "All of us have become like one who is unclean, and all our righteous acts are like filthy rags; we all shrivel up like a leaf, and like the wind our sins sweep us away" (Isaiah 64:6).

None have any claim to salvation. The most amazing thing is not that God doesn't save all but that He saves so many when all are guilty. To show love and mercy to some undeserving ones out of all the children of Adam is to truly see God's immense love demonstrated (Romans 5:8).

No, God does not give all an equal opportunity to be saved. Millions have never even heard the name of Jesus. This does not in any way incriminate God and put Him in a bad light. Rather, it magnifies His perfect jus-

[44] J. Zanchius and A. M. Toplady, *The Doctrine of Absolute Predestination* (Grand Rapids, MI: Baker Book House, 1977), 140.

tice toward sinners who deserve His justice and His immeasurable love to sinners who do not deserve His love. Many are perplexed at the statement in Romans 9:13, "Jacob have I loved, but Esau I hated." Instead of being disturbed over the fact that God hated Esau, I am amazed that God loved Jacob, as sinful as he was.

> For reasons known to Himself He sees that it is not best to pardon all, but that some should be permitted to have their own way and be left to eternal punishment in order that it may be shown what an awful thing is sin and rebellion against God.[45]

We must go to great pains to insist that salvation is by grace completely. Any mixture of works or human merit spoils it. It must be absolute or not at all. The very nature of grace demands it.

> So too, at the present time there is a remnant chosen by grace. And if by grace, then it is no longer by works; if it were, grace would no longer be grace (Romans 11:5–6).

The following statement by Boettner cannot be denied,

Arminianism destroys this purely gracious character of salvation and substitutes a system of grace plus works. No matter how small a part these works may play they are necessary and are the basis of the distinction between the saved and the lost and would then afford occasion for the saved to boast over the lost since each had equal opportunity. But Paul says that all boasting is excluded, and that he who glories should glory in the Lord (Romans 3:27; 1 Corinthians 1:31). But if saved by grace, the redeemed remembers the mire from which he was lifted, and his attitude toward the lost is one of sympathy and pity. He knows that but for the grace of God he too would have been in the same state as those who perish, and his song is, "Not unto us, O Lord, not unto us, but unto thy name give glory, for thy mercy and for thy truth's sake"[46]

---

[45] L. Boettner, *The Reformed Doctrine of Predestination* (New Jersey: Presbyterian and Reformed, 1932), 306.

[46] Ibid., 307.

8

The Sinfulness of Man

How sinful is man? How far did he fall when he fell into sin? Is he only sick or is he dead and unable to do anything to save himself? These are vital questions that must be given sound biblical answers. If we go astray here with a false presupposition and lay a cracked foundation, then the entire superstructure will be unstable. It is at this point that multitudes have erred and built doctrinal monstrosities.

The view an individual takes regarding man's sinfulness will determine his view of salvation. This point cannot be stressed too strongly. The reason there are all kinds of shallow, inadequate views of salvation is because of faulty ideas about man's condition before God. It is amazing how one's understanding of theology can improve simply by learning the basic facts about depravity.

Man by nature invariably does not want to acknowledge his desperate plight. He will inevitably evade the issue or make light of it. He does not want to see his helpless, hopeless condition. He will go to any lengths to make himself look good. He will deliberately devise religious systems and complicated ideologies to try and prove himself worthy.

No one likes to hear bad news. To hear the doctor's diagnoses of cancer or some other dread disease is not exactly pleasant news. How foolish we are, however, to deny it or not deal with it. In a similar way, the Bible calls all men sinners. "Your whole head is injured, your whole heart afflicted. From the sole of your foot to the top of your head there is no soundness—only wounds and welts and open sores, not cleansed or bandaged or soothed with oil" (Isaiah 1:5–6).

We are ruined and condemned with the worst kind of disease imaginable. It is the most awful news that has ever fallen on the ears of man. We must face it and admit our lostness. Our complete inability to do anything about our condition is exactly what we must see. Only in our utter help-lessness will we look away from ourselves and see the total adequacy and sufficiency of Christ, who alone can save.

People are so hardened in their own pride and self-righteousness that they will die and go to hell before admitting their lost condition and cast themselves completely on the mercy of God (Romans 1:32). The only thing that will cause a person to truly cry out to God to save him from his sinfulness is the drawing power of the Father (John 6:44).

One cannot understand or appreciate the doctrines of grace until he truly understands his depravity. When we see our total corruption and awful condemnation, and realize that only God can save a sinner, then we begin to understand something of His grace. Election must be uncondi-tional because man in his rebellion and arrogant stubbornness would never choose Christ. Stephen, in preaching to the self-righteous religious leaders of his day said something that is true of us all, "You always resist the Holy Spirit" (Acts 7:51).

Total depravity means that man is by nature corrupt, perverse and sin-ful throughout. This does not mean that man is as sinful as he possibly could be. Instead, it indicates that every part of man is contaminated by sin. The corruption extends to his body, mind and will.

I like G.I. Williamson's illustration in his commentary on the Shorter Catechism. Take three glasses and fill the first with pure water, represent-ing man without sin before the fall; fill the second with nothing but poi-son, representing sin and Satan as bad as they can be; and the third mixed with water and poison representing an accurate picture of man after the fall. Man is certainly not pure, but neither is he as bad as he can be. Instead, he is poisoned throughout. No one would drink the deadly water mixed with poison. Hence, man is not as poisoned as he could be but his purity is ruined and his corruption is sure.

Even the worst of people are capable of some relative good. Men are not as bad as they could be. Even Hitler, Stalin and other notorious politi-cal criminals performed deeds that people would call good. Sinful men can possess admirable qualities. There are those who sometimes overwhelm us with exceptional acts of kindness, but are still in bondage to sin and dark-ness. Dr. Albert Schweitzer is an example of this. History has shown us few men as benevolent and self-giving as he. Yet, he denied the deity of Christ.

Man's sinfulness means he is incapable of doing any spiritual good or works acceptable to God. "All of us have become like one who is unclean, and all our righteous acts are like filthy rags; we all shrivel up like a leaf, and like the wind our sins sweep us away" (Isaiah 64:6). Our best efforts are not worthy of God's approval. We are all bankrupt sinners with no ability to save ourselves.

Let's not make the terrible mistake of imagining sinful man as naturally loving Christ and longing to come to Him but just can't quite achieve it. It is foolishness indeed to think that all man needs is just some assistance. "The sinful mind is hostile to God. It does not submit to God's law, nor can it do so. Those controlled by the sinful nature cannot please God" (Romans 8:7–8).

By nature man is a God-hating, Christ-rejecting, Spirit-resisting, sin-loving rebel as shown in the following verses:

> You belong to your father, the devil, and you want to carry out your father's desires (John 8:44).

> You were dead in your transgressions and sins, in which you used to live when you followed the ways of this world and of the ruler of the kingdom of the air, the spirit who is now at work in those who are disobedient. All of us also lived among them at one time, gratifying the cravings of our sinful nature and following its desires and thoughts. Like the rest, we were by nature objects of wrath (Ephesians 2:1–3).

> While we were still sinners, Christ died for us (Romans 5:8).

Does that sound like people want to come to Christ? No! Man loves his sin and obstinately "shakes his fist" in the face of God. We are in a state of rebellion, running from God. Man in his sinfulness does not seek God. Listen to the way Paul describes this:

> There is no one righteous, not even one; there is no one who understands, no one who seeks God. All have turned away, they have together become worthless; there is no one who does good, not even one. Their throats are open graves; their tongues practice deceit. The poison of vipers is on their lips. Their mouths are full of cursing and bitterness. Their feet are swift to shed blood; ruin and misery mark their ways, and the way of peace they do not know. There is no fear of God before their eyes....for all have sinned and fall short of the glory of God (Romans 3:10–18 and 23).

Even a superficial reading of this passage will quickly reveal that man needs far more than a little assistance to come to Christ. He needs resurrection! Genesis 6:5 reveals much in helping us understand the nature of man:

> The Lord saw how great man's wickedness on the earth had become, and that every inclination of the thoughts of his heart was only evil all the time.

Our wickedness is inward and spills out from our hearts. We tend to minimize our sin and think there is not enough there to get upset about. We excuse ourselves. But God sees our wickedness and looks upon it as totally corrupt.

It is also universal and continual in that it spreads to everyone in every place and in every generation. Consider the following texts:

> What comes out of a man is what makes him "unclean." For from within, out of men's hearts, come evil thoughts, sexual immorality, theft, murder, adultery, greed, malice, deceit, lewdness. envy, slander, arrogance, and folly. All these evils come from inside and make a man "unclean" (Mark 7:20–23).

> Every inclination of his heart is evil from childhood (Genesis 8:21).

> Even from birth the wicked go astray; from the womb they are wayward and speak lies (Psalm 58:3).

> Surely I was sinful at birth, sinful from the time my mother conceived me (Psalm 51:5).

> The hearts of men…are full of evil and there is madness in their hearts while they live (Ecclesiasties 9:3).

> The heart is deceitful above all things and beyond cure. Who can understand it? (Jeremiah 17:9).

> This is the verdict: Light has come into the world, but men loved darkness instead of light because their deeds were evil (John 3:19).

> The man without the Spirit does not accept the things that come from the Spirit of God, for they are foolishness to him, and he cannot understand them, because they are spiritually discerned (1 Corinthians 2:14).

These texts are just a few of many that unequivocally show how sinful men are. Total depravity is the only true biblical position. When we try to argue that man is still capable of doing something to save himself, it is simply another deceptively subtle way human nature has of cleverly covering its inward corruption.

A very important key in grasping what the Bible teaches concerning human sinfulness is to see our oneness with respect to Adam and all the members of the human race. We are all children of Adam as these verses reveal:

> Therefore, just as sin entered the world through one man, and death through sin, and in this way death came to all men, because all sinned… by the trespass of the one man (Adam), death reigned through that one man….just as the result of one trespass was condemnation for all men…. For just as through the disobedience of the one man the many were made sinners (Romans 5:12,17,18 and 19).

The Bible also says:

> From one man he made every nation of men, that they should inhabit the whole earth (Acts 17:26).

Every descendant of Adam takes on his corrupted nature. Therefore, such texts as these come into focus:

> Who can bring what is pure from the impure? No one! and how then can man be righteous before God? How can one born of woman be pure? (Job 14:4, 25:4).

> Even from birth the wicked go astray; from the womb they are wayward and speak lies (Psalm 58:3).

These Scriptures make us ask the age old question, "Why does God blame me for what Adam did? I wasn't even there! God forces on me something I did not want." Jesus' illustration about trees and their fruit gives us light on this subject:

> No good tree bears bad fruit, nor does a bad tree bear good fruit. Each tree is recognized by its own fruit. People do not pick figs from thorn bushes, or grapes from briers. The good man brings good things out of the good stored up in his heart, and the evil man brings evil things out of the evil stored up in his heart. For out of the overflow of his heart his mouth speaks (Luke 6:43–45).

Just as no good fruit can come from a bad tree, neither can any good come from man's sinful nature, which we inherited from Adam. He was the tree and we are the branches. The fruit that comes from this tree of the human race cannot produce anything good. When a tree is first planted there is no fruit until later. When Adam was placed in the Garden we were not yet in existence. Adam, being the father of the human race, acted for the human race as our representative. Adam's sin is our sin. Because of this we share his penalty of death.

With a little thought, anyone can understand the meaning of representation. For instance, the people in any given state act in and through their representatives in political office. The decisions the representative make, whether good or bad, affect those he represents.

A president and others in Washington make decisions every day that will affect the entire nation. Parents act as representatives of their children. To a great degree they decide the destinies of their offspring. If they set good examples in honesty, integrity, morality and faithfulness then the children will benefit. But the children suffer if there is a mom or dad who is immoral, dishonest or abusive. There are worlds of illustrations of this representative principle that operate in different ways in everyday life. Hence, it is not hard at all to see this in Scripture. Indeed, Adam did stand as the official representative of the entire human race. We, as those he represented have to share the effects of his sin.

It is argued by some that if they had been put under the same situation as Adam, they would not have sinned. It must be remembered that Adam was created upright (Ecclesiasties 7:29). Hence, his will was not in bondage to a sinful nature as ours. If he made a wrong choice when created righteous, how do we think we could do better when we are born enslaved to sin?

Another thing we must ever keep in mind is that God has declared it to be so, even though we may not understand it. I never have the right to change what God's Word teaches because I don't like or understand it. We must always let the Bible speak. It is abundantly clear in Scripture that we all have sinned in Adam and share the same penalty. Like it or not, that's the way it is. We must deal with it.

Instead of yelling, "Unfair, unfair!" consider Christ, who is our second Adam, and find forgiveness for the sin you inherited. After all, it says in Romans 5:17–19,

> For if, by the trespass of the one man, death reigned through that one
> man, how much more will those who receive God's abundant provi-

sion of grace and of the gift of righteousness reign in life through the one man, Jesus Christ. Consequently, just as the result of one trespass was condemnation for all men, so also the result of one act of righteousness was justification that brings life for all men. For just as through the disobedience of the one man the many were made sinners, so also through the obedience of the one man the many will be made righteous.

If we fail to understand our part in the first Adam's act of sin, by which we fell, we also will fail to understand our part in the second Adam's (Christ) act of righteousness, by which we are saved. Many died in Adam (the whole human race). Many also are made alive in Christ (all who believe in Him—the elect). We like the part that says we are made alive in Christ, but we don't like the part about being dead in Adam's sin. However, we cannot separate these two truths. If we accept the one we like, we must also accept the other that we don't like in order to be in harmony with Scripture.

Instead of stubbornly resisting this truth and running from your Creator, why not turn to Christ who died for sinners? Confess your sins and total helplessness. He is our only hope. If you are looking for another way out, you will never find it. Please don't try to cover your sins. Cry to Him for mercy. Be aware that a look of faith will save. "Just as Moses lifted the snake in the desert, so the Son of Man must be lifted up, that everyone who believes in him may have eternal life" (John 3:14–15). Look away from yourself and your sin to Christ. Turn your back on all that you are depending on for salvation and "turn to me and be saved, all you ends of the earth; for I am God, and there is no other" (Isaiah 45:22). There is every reason to believe He will save you. "Everyone who calls on the name of the Lord will be saved" (Romans 10:13).

9

The Free Will of Man

Most people tenaciously cling to the belief that man has free will. Very quickly people will stand to defend it. Arguments, conflicts and divisions have frequently occurred over this subject throughout church history. Numerous times it has been argued, "Has God not given man the power to decide his destiny? We're not robots! Isn't free will the key to the power of the human soul? Surely all men have the ability to make decisions and choices!"

In my early years as a preacher, I held the popular belief about free will, that man's fall into sin did not extend all the way to his will. I was never taught anything else nor did I give serious thought to other views. In those days, I tended to avoid issues that my "preacher idols" avoided.

However, I believed the doctrine of total depravity, or at least I thought I did. My mistake was that I had never studied it deeply enough to discern all it meant. I naively thought that man, in cooperation with the mere as-sistance of the Holy Spirit, has the power of self-determination and can freely will to do that which is good and acceptable in the sight of God. Ev-eryone I had known believed this, especially preachers. Hence, for several years I didn't question it. Little did I know that man needs far more than the mere assistance of the Spirit. He needs regeneration or resurrection from spiritual death before he can respond positively to the gospel by true repentance and faith or even see his need to respond.

I believed very strongly in "decisionism" and that man's "free will" pre-ceded God's will in initiating the new birth. I believed God could do very little for man until man "let" Him save him. The ironic thing was that I had a very strong belief in the inerrant Word of God and sincerely thought I was being true to it.

My preaching was done in such a way as to get people "down the aisle." The preacher who could get the most people to make decisions was the most successful and most sought after for revivals. Whether or not there were "visible results" determined how successful a worship service was. I greatly admired preachers who could preach to thousands and see hundreds respond to the invitation. I found myself trying to imitate them.

This is not to say that I do not believe in urgently and zealously inviting people to come to Christ and deciding for Him. It is to say, however, that I believe in honoring the sovereign work of the Spirit in regeneration. Our missionary and evangelistic efforts should always be to compassionately plead with men to repent and come to Christ. But the wise Christian witness will never try to take the place of the Spirit by getting people to make decisions for Christ before the Father has done His work of drawing them (John 6:44). It is because of the violation of this principle that we have scores of people in our churches who have been decisioned but not saved.

In my study of Scripture I finally came to see that I had swallowed an enormous lie that Satan has perpetrated on the human race for centuries. It is so widespread and almost universally believed that it is difficult to get a fair hearing. As a matter of fact, the God-centered gospel of sovereign grace has been so grossly neglected over the past seventy five to one hundred years that the whole Arminian system has become a stronghold of unbelievable proportions. Whether we're willing to admit it or not, human nature is such that we will inevitably cling to that which will flatter us or boost our pride. Nothing but the supernatural power of God can open our eyes and reveal the truth to us.

The position one takes relative to free will is pivotal in determining whether he believes the gospel is man-centered or God-centered. It is at the very heart of the Arminian versus Calvinism controversy.

Some clarifications are necessary in order to insure a proper understanding of this subject and to disarm those who assume we Calvinists believe people are robots. First of all, there is a difference between free will and being morally responsible. All of us are morally responsible. This simply means that man has a will. He obviously has the power to make decisions, choices, and determine his course of action. This is also called free agency. *The Baptist Faith And Message* states under article V, "Election is the gracious purpose of God.... It is consistent with the *free agency* of man, and comprehends all the means in connection with the end" (emphasis mine). Man is a free agent but he does not have free will. We must understand the difference. The two are not to be confused.

Man's choices are always conditioned by his sinful nature. He is free to act but he always acts according to his nature. He does not make choices outside the realm of who he is. Part of what total depravity means is that man, after the Fall, was rendered powerless to accomplish any spiritual good. This is called *total inability*. To grasp this important truth, one must realize that man fell in Adam all the way to his death: "Therefore, just as sin entered the world through one man (Adam), and death through sin, and in this way death came to all men, because all sinned" (Romans 5:12). He is completely deaf and blind spiritually. Man is no more able to save himself than a dead man is able to raise himself, nor is he able to prepare himself for resurrection by an act of his will. Would a sinner—rebellious, hard-hearted, arrogant, self-righteous, sin loving—ever want to come to Christ and give up his precious idols? Of course not! How could he, in light of the fact that everything in his nature runs contrary to the gospel?

The gospel demands repentance, self-denial, holiness and supreme love to God. Without a complete change of nature it is impossible for an unholy child of wrath to deny self, take up his cross and follow Christ.

Man's problem is not his will but his heart. Here are some verses that show this:

> The heart is deceitful above all things and beyond cure. Who can understand it? (Jeremiah 17:9).

> What comes out of a man is what makes him "unclean." For from within, out of men's hearts, come evil thoughts, sexual immorality, theft, murder, adultery, greed, malice, deceit, lewdness, envy, slander, arrogance and folly. All these evils come from inside and make a man "unclean" (Mark 7:20–23).

People have asked me, after discovering I am a Calvinist, "Don't you believe in John 3:16?" My reply is, "Yes, with all my heart. But I also believe in John 3:19."

> This is the verdict: Light has come into the world, but men loved darkness instead of light because their deeds were evil (John 3:19).

Until a man's heart is changed, he will continue to love the darkness and hate the light.

Dr. Donald Gray Barnhouse, the outstanding preacher, writer and former pastor of the Tenth Presbyterian Church in Philadelphia, gives this illustration about the absurdity of a dead sinner wanting Christ. Imagine a dead man lying in a coffin and his hand hanging out the side. Though dead, could he still have the ability to motion with his hand for someone to come to him? It is ridiculous to think so. It is just as absurd to imagine someone dead in trespasses and sins (Ephesians 2:1) to have even the slightest desire to call Christ to himself for salvation.

Ponder these clear words from the mouth of our Lord Himself:

> Make a tree good and its fruit will be good, or make a tree bad and its fruit will be bad, for a tree is recognized by its fruit. You brood of vipers, how can you who are evil say anything good? For out of the overflow of the heart the mouth speaks. The good man brings good things out of the good things stored up in him, and the evil man brings evil things out of the evil stored up in him. But I tell you that men will have to give account on the day of judgment for every careless word they have spoken. For by your words you will be acquitted, and by your words you will be condemned (Matthew 12:33–37).

Bad fruit trees produce bad fruit. Good fruit trees produce good fruit. Here Jesus makes a very easy to understand point. The kind of choices we make always reflects what is in our hearts. No one makes an evil man do evil. He desires to do so. Neither is a good man coerced to do good. Sin reaches down to man's ability to make decisions. His choices always reflect what is in his heart; therefore, he will not choose that which is distasteful to his normal appetites.

The illustration of the cow and the buzzard gives clarity. Cows love hay and grain. They will not eat decayed meat, as buzzards do. You can try as you will to get a cow to eat what is distasteful to his normal appetite and he will turn it down every time. As a matter of fact, he will starve before he will eat it. On the other hand, a buzzard will eat decayed meat and never touch hay or grain. Why? Because it is his nature. It is not that a cow or buzzard *can't* eat each other's food. Technically, they could. The fact is, they will not.

Suppose someone demanded that you stab your best friend with a knife. Your immediate response would be that you could not do such a thing. The fact is that you *would* not. Technically, you could if you so desired but because you love that friend and value his life, you would not.

I like all kinds of food. My appetite is such that I will eat almost anything edible. But there are a few things I do not like, such as raw celery, cooked carrots, etc. It's not that I can't eat them. I could if I would, but I just don't like them.

The reason for man's inability to come to Christ is because of his stubborn will. His natural sin-loving appetite won't let him. He is unable to come because he will not come. He could if he would but his "would" is bound to his sin which he loves so much. By nature the gospel is distasteful to him. He would much rather give his time, energy, money, talent, yea, even his very life to that which pleases his natural desires. Man has "free will" all right; he always freely chooses sin. He freely decides to gratify his self-centered disposition.

God never forces His will on anyone as some seem to think. In the *London Baptist Confession* in paragraph 1 of chapter 3: "God's Decrees" we read,

> God hath decreed in himself, from all eternity, by the most wise and holy counsel of his own will, freely and unchangeably, all things whatsoever comes to pass; yet so as thereby is God neither the author of sin, nor hath fellowship with any therein, nor is violence offered to the will of the creature, nor yet is the liberty, or contingency of second causes taken away, but rather established.

And in chapter 9 "Of Free Will" it states,

> God hath endued the will of man with that natural liberty and power of acting upon choice, that it is neither forced, nor by any necessity of nature determined to do good or evil. Man, in his state of innocency had freedom, and power, to will, and to do, that which was good, and well-pleasing to God; but yet was mutable, so that he might fall from it. Man, by his fall unto a state of sin, hath wholly lost all ability of will, to any spiritual good accompanying salvation; so as a natural man, being altogether averse from that good and dead in sin, is not able, by his own strength, to convert himself or to prepare himself there unto. When God converts a sinner, and translates him into the state of grace, he freeth him from his natural bondage under sin, and by his grace alone, enables him freely to will, and do that which is spiritually good; yet so as that by reason of his remaining corruptions, he doth not perfectly nor only will that which is good, but doth also will that which is evil. The will of man is made perfectly and immutably free to good alone in the state of glory only.

How marvelously taught of God our Baptist forefathers were!

10

The Doctrine of Election

That the doctrine of election is taught in the Bible is without question. Anyone who studies the Scripture will readily see that words such as *election*, *elect* and *chosen* are commonly used. If you believe the Bible, you must believe in the doctrine of election. The big question is not *if* it is taught in Scripture but *how* it is taught.

There are three big reasons why there is so much misunderstanding about the doctrine of election. First, because it is understated. It is so "watered down" by most that it has little or no substance at all. When many teachers and preachers get through with it, it has lost all its strength and significance. Arminianism appears today in all sorts of forms and in varying degrees. In various ways it contributes to the destruction of this wonderful doctrine of grace.

Second, because it is overstated. There are those that are hyper-Calvinists. Some call it "Hardshellism." This is not as prevalent today as it once was. It does not give proper balance to the responsibility of man and the sovereignty of God. It is fatalistic, unevangelistic and anti-missions. This is just as dangerous on the one hand as Arminianism is on the other.

Third, because it is not stated at all. Dr. John Carter, long time professor at Clarke College in Newton, Mississippi, outstanding Southern Baptist and outspoken Calvinist wrote *A Layman's Manual of Christian Doctrines*. He made this statement:

> A study of the doctrine of election in regard to God's bestowal of salvation is evaded as much as possible by many people. Either the acceptance or the rejection of it is fraught with perplexing difficulties, both exegetical and philosophical. It seems to me, however, that the difficulties attending the rejection of the doctrine are greater than those attending its

acceptance. We can only confess that in this matter, as in many others, the ways of God are past tracing out (Romans 11:33).[47]

Many do not even have a belief about election. For many years I did not because I never studied it. It was not until only a few years ago that I ever heard a sermon on election. As important as it is, I have often been amazed that it is spoken of so little. Many seminary trained and seasoned pastors cannot give a sound biblical explanation of election. Such foreboding tones are often sounded with reference to it that many are scared away and told not to use that awful "E" word. One might get the idea that it is top secret information. It is quickly passed off as too deep and controversial to discuss, much less be the subject of a sermon.

Several years ago I heard one of our leading Southern Baptists preachers deliver a sermon in which he sought to refute Calvinism. He grossly misrepresented it. It was obvious he had not done his homework. He simply raised up the caricatures, not the truth, and proceeded to tear them down. This seems to be typical of several mega church preachers across our Convention, whose word with some is unquestioned, that the doctrines of grace have suffered such terrible abuse.

I am convinced that election is much like the early Christians that were cruelly persecuted by being wrapped in animal skins to serve as appetizers for the wild dogs to devour. Election has suffered severe and unjust persecution. Hence, it is essential to first disarm prejudice and clear away the rubbish in order to get to the truth. Therefore I would first like to tell what election is *not*:

(1) It is *not* conditional. This is the widespread view that says election is based on foreseen faith or works. According to this belief, God, in eternity, looked down through the ages and saw who would repent and believe when presented the gospel. Hence, He chose those whom He foresaw would believe. Apparently this is reasonable to many because of its popularity. A careful analysis, however, will expose serious error.

First of all, it denies what the Bible says about man's sinful nature and the bondage of the will. "The man without the Spirit does not accept the things that come from the Spirit of God, for they are foolishness to him, and he cannot understand them, because they are spiritually discerned" (1 Corinthians 2:14).

---

[47] J. F. Carter, *A Layman's Manual of Christian Doctrine* (Mississippi: Author, 1972), 354.

Man cannot repent and believe. These are grace gifts (Acts 5:13 and 11:18; 2 Timothy, 2:25; Ephesians 2:8–10; 1 Corinthians 3:5–9). God did not foresee these things in the sinner because the sinner does not have them. If God waited on people to chose Him first, He would be waiting forever. Of course God sees and knows everything, including who will be saved. However, all He sees in the sinner is nothing but continual sin (Genesis 6:5). Man's wicked heart extends all the way to his will. The Lord must change the rebellious heart of man in order for him to savingly desire the gospel (Zechariah 4:6; John 1:13; Romans 9:16).

It is argued that man is created in the image of God and stands in "awesome freedom" to decide his own destiny in the light of God's offer of salvation. It is said that the very nature of God is love and the offer of salvation is an offer of love. Love does not force or coerce. Therefore, man has to be free to make his own decisions. But there is nothing in Calvinism that says man is forced to be saved. God does not grab and pull someone into salvation kicking and screaming against his will.

Second, it makes some better than others. If conditional election is espoused, then total honesty must admit human pride. Superior knowledge and righteousness must be claimed if this view is believed. The Bible says we are all children of wrath and come from the same lump of clay (Ephesians 2:3; Romans 9:21). There is no difference, for all have sinned and come short of the glory of God (Romans 3:23). None could be saved had the Lord not shown grace to some. As someone once said to me, "Man, left to himself, does not have sense enough to be saved." How true!

Third, it makes the basis of election to be in the sinner and his choice rather than in God's purpose of grace and sovereign choice. Election is based upon the good pleasure of His will and to the praise of the glory of His grace (Ephesians 1:4–6). To say that God chooses to save if and when man chooses to be saved takes the entire meaning and strength out of the doctrine of election altogether. It is never presented in Scripture as man choosing God first but God choosing man (John 15:16). We love Him because He first loved us (1 John 4:19).

Fourth, it perverts the biblical meaning of foreknowledge. Many will invariably make this statement, "I know God knows who will be saved because He knows all things. Therefore God elects on the basis of whom He knows will believe." However, this reflects an inadequate view of foreknowledge and will always mislead. It means far more than a mere knowledge of future events and persons. Wayne Grudem, in his *Systematic Theol-*

ogy, gives the following explanation of foreknowledge in commenting on Romans 8:29:

> But this verse can hardly be used to demonstrate that God based his predestination on foreknowledge of the fact that a person would believe. The passage speaks rather of the fact that God knew persons ("those whom he foreknew"), not that he knew some fact about them, such as the fact that they would believe. It is a personal, relational knowledge that is spoken of here: God, looking into the future, thought of certain people in saving relationship to him, and in that sense he "knew them" long ago. This is the sense in which Paul can talk about God's "knowing" someone, for example, in I Corinthians 8:3: "But if one love God, one is known by him." Similarly, he says "but now that you have come to know God, or rather to be known by God...."(Gal.4:9). When people know God in Scripture, or when God knows them, it is personal knowledge that involoves a saving relationship. Therefore in Romans 8:29, "those whom he foreknew" is best understood to mean, "those whom he long ago thought of in a saving relationship to himself." The text actually says nothing about God foreknowing or foreseeing that certain people would believe, nor is that idea mentioned in any other text of Scripture.[48]

(2) It is *not* the Hobbs "Category" interpretation. Although this is a form of conditional election, of which the above objections also apply, I want to treat it separately because of its popularity among Southern Baptists.

Dr. Herchel Hobbs has been called the "Patron Saint" among Southern Baptists. He was an outstanding preacher and writer. It may very well be that more Southern Baptists have read him on a regular basis than any other Southern Baptist writer because for many years he wrote quarterly commentaries in the Life and Work Sunday School lesson series. He has also written several other valuable commentaries. He chaired The Baptist Faith and Message Committee that updated our Statement of Faith in 1963, about which he also wrote a commentary. Many years ago, as a young Christian, I listened regularly with great profit to Dr. Hobbs on "The Baptist Hour." We owe him an enormous debt for his many contributions to Southern Baptists life.

[48] Wayne Grudem, *Systematic Theology* (Grand Rapids, MI, 1994), 676-677.

However, he has not served us well in his rendition of election. Many Southern Baptists have embraced it simply because "Dr. Hobbs taught it." It goes like this:

> ...Ephesians 1:3–13, Paul's most complete treatment of election. Note the words "hath chosen" and "having predestinated" in verses 4–5. The former translates the Greek verb for elect. So God "elected us in him before the foundation of the world." "Predestinated" translates a verb meaning to mark out the boundaries beforehand (see v. 11). But note also that God has chosen "in him." Thus God's election was in Christ. And he marked out the boundaries of salvation in love, not by an arbitrary choice.
> Against this background it is well to note that in eleven verses Paul used the phrase "in Christ" or its equivalent ten times. So God has chosen "in the sphere of Christ." He elected that all who are "in Christ" shall be saved. "In Christ" is the boundary that God marked out beforehand, like building a fence around a field. God did this in his sovereignty. In this act he asked the counsel or permission of no one. All who are within the fence "in Christ" shall be saved.
> Man is free to choose whether or not he will be in Christ. This does not mean that man can boast of his salvation once he chooses Christ. It is the result of God's initiative and saving purpose. Man receives this inheritance because God marked out the boundaries of salvation beforehand according to the counsel of his own will (v.11). Thus it should be to the praise of his glory that men had a hope beforehand (v. 12) in Christ.
> But at this point Paul took care of man's free will. It is seen in the passage "in whom also after that ye believed" (v. 13). Paul's readers heard the gospel of salvation that all who are "in Christ" shall be saved. They could have rejected it and remained in a lost condition. But they believed "in Christ" and thus were saved. That God knew beforehand who would believe is obvious. But, as previously stated, foreknowledge of an event does not cause it.
> God never violates human personality. He will not save a man against his will. He knocks at the door of the heart, but he will not force it to open. However, to all who of their own wills will open the door, he enters and saves graciously apart from man's own efforts or merits.[49]

Dr. Nettles comments that Hobbs' view causes unconditional election to suffer an unmitigated rejection in favor of a conditional election

---

[49] H. H. Hobbs, *The Baptist Faith and Message* (Nashville, TN: Convention Press, 1971), 66-67.

of categories, not people. He gives five reasons that soundly refute Hobbs'
position. If Hobbs is believed then:

1. Free will eats up divine sovereignty.

2. Election concerns a category rather than persons. Hobbs says, "So God
    elected that all who 'are in Christ' will be saved. All outside of Christ
    will be lost." This position must certainly be regarded as true, as far as it
    goes, but it ignores the truth that persons as individuals are the objects
    of God's electing love. God considers them as in Christ rather than the
    category "in Christ" apart from the individuals contemplated as being
    in that position. A careful exegesis of Ephesians 1:3–13 will not support
    this view, nor does any other text in the Bible even hint to such a belief,
    such as Romans 8:29, "For *those* God foreknew he also predestined to
    be conformed to the likeness of his Son, that he might be the firstborn
    among many brothers." It was *persons* upon whom He set His love in
    advance, not a mere impersonal knowledge, nor a category of people.

3. Belief loses its gracious character and becomes synonymous with "free
    will."

4. Foreknowledge is changed from predetermination to mere cognizance of
    events before they occur.

5. The final cause in the effecting of redemption is the will of man: Hobbs
    says, "The final choice lay with man. God in his sovereignty set the con-
    dition. Man in his free will determines the result."[50]

As invaluable as most of Dr. Hobbs writings are, we must respectfully
reject his "Category" interpretation of divine election.

(3) It is *not* salvation but unto salvation.

> But we ought always to thank God for you, brothers loved by the
> Lord, because from the beginning God chose you to be saved through
> the sanctifying work of the Spirit and through belief in the truth
> (1 Thessalonians 2:13).

---

[50] Thomas J. Nettles, *By His Grace and For His Glory* (Cape Coral, FL:
Founders Press, 2006), 236–237.

In the light of this text, election must precede salvation. We are not elected when we believe, as many falsely think. It is nonsense to speak of someone being elected to have something he already has. We are saved when we believe, therefore, election at that point would not be necessary. Election took place in eternity before the creation of the world. Salvation takes place in time, when the sinner repents and believes. It is not because God saw faith and repentance in some and on that basis chose them. Faith and repentance cannot be the cause of election.

Salvation comes when the sanctifying work of the Spirit and belief of the truth are accomplished, not before. From the beginning (before the creation of the world), we are chosen to be saved. People are saved when they repent and believe, not when they are elected. Just as a political official is elected before he is actually placed into office, so the believer is elected long before he is made a saint by the work of the Spirit who calls him to salvation. Election is first, then salvation comes when one believes.

(4) It is *not* "God has voted for you, the Devil has voted against you and you cast the deciding vote." Among some, this is a very common and popular statement. However, this implies that God and the Devil are equals. One seems to appear to be just as powerful as the other. But the Devil is not even a qualified voter, much less remotely equal with God in strength. It is also very presumptuous. It falsely assumes and naively believes that man is able to see clearly and look objectively at both sides and make the right choice. The Bible and common sense simply will not support this. To believe this is yet another example of how countless numbers of people inevitably forget to take into consideration the inborn inability of man to do anything of spiritual good. Man is spiritually blind, deaf, dumb and dead. He is an incurably biased, uninformed voter. He will invariably cast his vote in favor of his father the Devil (John 8:44).

(5) It is *not* the cause of anyone going to hell. Remember, it is election unto salvation. It is a doctrine of grace, not a deterrent to it. Neither is non-election responsible for the damnation of sinners. It is sin in the hearts of mankind that condemns. God is not the culprit. It is man and his love for sin. It does not shut the door of salvation, but opens that door for all those who come to Christ. Election harms no one. Anyone who wants to be saved certainly can be. Ernest Reisinger says,

> A very important distinction must be made between a mere desire to escape hell and a desire to be saved from sin. The desire to be saved from hell is a natural desire—no one wants to burn. The desire to be saved from sin is a spiritual desire and is a result of the convicting work of the

Holy Spirit—God's electing grace is the mother of this desire to be saved
from sin (John 6:37, 44, 63, 65; 10:9; 14:6).[51]

(6) It is *not* the destruction of man's so-called *free will*. The will of man
is normally defined as that which he naturally desires, wishes or chooses.
However, his choice is always sin. He *freely* chooses what his nature desires.
Only by God's grace do men freely come to Christ. Lazarus *freely* began
to rot in the tomb until Jesus called him forth out of the grave. Because
Christ called him to life, he was able to freely come to Him. That's the way
it always is with God's elect (John 3:19, 20; 5:40; 3:11; 2:2, 3; 4:17–19;
Jeremiah 17:9; 13:23; Psalm 65:4; 110:3; John 6:44, 65; Acts 13:48; John
11).

(7) It is *not* fatalism, but is the work of God. Fatalism is a very imper-
sonal philosophy that says, "whatever will be will be" so why try or exert
any initiative? The Bible and common sense refute such a thought. Yes,
God does work all things after the counsel of His own will (Ephesians
1:11), but it is whatever God says will be. He has decreed all things that
come to pass. But there is nothing in the Bible that discourages human initiative and responsibility. Rather, it is upheld from Genesis to Revelation.
While we cannot earn His salvation, we are still admonished to seek, work,
strive, obey, repent, believe and even force (1 Thessalonians 1:4; Matthew
6:33; Ephesians 2:8–10; Philippians 2:12–13; Matthew 11:12).

(8) It is *not* injustice on God's part. It is not unjust for God to save
an unnumbered multitude of unworthy sinners in His mercy and to justly
leave others in their sins. God is never obligated to save anyone. He is
perfectly righteous and just to let sinners go in their sins and receive the
punishment they deserve. If a governor pardons one convict, is it injustice
to leave the rest, who justly deserve to be punished for their crime, unpar-
doned? Of course not! If a benevolent man goes to a reform school and
adopts a boy as his own to love, train and provide for, would he be unjust
to leave the rest who justly deserve to be there? Certainly not!

God chose not to save the fallen angels. They were sent to gloomy
dungeons to be held for judgment (2 Peter 2:4). Was He unjust in doing
so? Not at all. They will be judged with perfect righteousness and justly
condemned. Just because the devil and his demons are incapable of repentance and righteousness in no way excuses them. They are hardened

[51] Ernest Reisinger, *A Southern Baptist Looks at the Biblical Doctrine of Election* (Cape Coral, FL: Founders Press, 2000), 8.

in their rebellion, and God would be unjust if He did not bring judgment upon them. Should a kleptomaniac be excused from punishment because he can't resist the temptation to steal? Would a just judge excuse him because he says he can't help it? Obviously not! Neither will God excuse sinners on the basis of their inability to obey Him. They are responsible for their actions and will be reckoned with accordingly.

Besides, when careful thought is given to this matter, it makes salvation a divine obligation. It would obligate God the Creator to man the sinful creature. If man deserved justice then God would be unjust not to give salvation to all. It would take away the right of the potter (represented as God) over the clay (represented as man):

> What then shall we say? Is God unjust? Not at all! For he says to Moses, "I will have mercy on whom I have mercy, and I will have compassion on whom I have compassion." It does not, therefore, depend on man's desire or effort, but on God's mercy....Therefore God has mercy on whom he wants to have mercy, and he hardens whom he wants to harden. One of you will say to me: "Then why does God still blame us? For who resists his will?" But who are you, O man, to talk back to God? "Shall what is formed say to him who formed it, 'Why did you make me like this?'"Does not the potter have the right to make out of the same lump of clay some pottery for noble purposes and some for common use? (Romans 9:14–16, 18–21).

It was God's love, mercy and grace that led to salvation in the first place, not justice. If individuals get what they justly deserve, they would go to hell and have no one to blame but themselves. If they go to heaven, they would have no one but God to praise.

Now I would like to state what election *is*.

(1) It *is* unconditional. Dr. Carter gives the following excellent definition of biblical election:

> As pertains to the bestowal of salvation, election is God's choosing in eternity past, according to the principles of His sovereign love, wisdom, and righteousness, of certain individuals from among the race of sinful humanity, without regard to any foreseen merit or lack of merit in them,

to be the objects of the Holy Spirit's regenerating grace, and thus volun-
tarily to become the recipients of salvation in Christ.[52]

Consider again the statement in *The Baptist Faith and Message* relative
to election, "Election is the gracious purpose of God, according to which
He regenerates, sanctifies, and glorifies sinners..." Also, Article V from
the *Abstract of Principles*, the official definition of election adopted by The
Southern Baptist Theological Seminary on April 30, 1858:

> Election is God's eternal choice of some persons unto everlasting life—
> not because of foreseen merit in them, but of His mere mercy in Christ—
> in consequence of which choice they are called, justified, and glorified.

There is no question as to how early Southern Baptists stood on this
doctrine. All the Old Baptist confessions of faith that shaped our convention, such as, *The Baptist Confession of 1689* (London Confession), *The
Philadelphia Confession of 1742* and *The New Hampshire Confession*, emphatically declare the blessed doctrine of sovereign election.

My good friend Charles Rosson, outstanding Southern Baptist evangelist for many years from Arkansas and one who has faithfully held to
and unashamedly preached the doctrines of grace, when it was even more
unpopular than now, wrote the following unique explanation that clarifies
unconditional election:

> **Are you one of God's elect poeple?** Some people say they have problems
> with the grand, God-honoring doctrine of scriptural election. Having
> read and heard most, if not all, the things people say in opposition to this
> doctrine, let me remind you that the Bible is full of it. No individual can
> claim to believe the Bible and disbelieve the teaching that exalts God
> and humbles us more than any other in the Scriptures. The following
> four questions will help you and, in turn, allow you to help others when
> discussing the doctrine of election:
>
> 1. *Did you save yourself or did God save you?* All true believers who know
>   their Bibles will immediately reply that God, in His infinite mercy, saved
>   them. All believers who "search the Scriptures" renounce all claims of
>   self merit or human works as either producing or preserving their right
>   standing with God. Our eternal salvation is of God! (Ephesians 2:8–
>   10).

---

[52] Carter, *A Layman's Manual*, 354-355.

2. *Did God save you on purpose or by accident?* Eventually all true believers who know their Bibles recognize that our eternal, sovereign, all-wise God does nothing—absolutely nothing—by accident. His creation of the universe and all that is in it, including the human race, was by His design. And our redemption, requiring the death of His Son, was part of His eternal plan and purpose (Romans 8:28–39).

3. *When did God plan to save you?* The day you trusted Him? The day you cried or joined the church or was baptized? The Bibles says He chose us "before the creation of the world" (Ephesians 1:3–13, 2 Thessalonians 2:13).

4. *Why did God plan to save you?* While many will agree with all the above, they get very confused at this point. Did God plan to save you because you are a member of a certain race or family? More intelligent? Morally superior? Better looking? The Bible says that we might be "holy and blameless in His sight" (Ephesians 1:4, Phi. 2:12–13, Titus 2:11–14).

In a sentence: God saves sinners on purpose according to His eternal plan that they might be His holy people![53]

(2) It *is* a doctrine of grace. Without election, no one would be saved. God's salvation would only be a dream, not a reality. A mere outward invitation brings nobody to Christ.

"So too, at the present time there is a remnant chosen by grace. And if by grace, then it is no longer by works; if it were, grace would no longer be grace" (Romans 11:5–6). Ernest Reisinger says,

The attitude of men toward election is the acid test of their belief in salvation by grace. Those who oppose election cannot consistently claim to believe in salvation by grace. A simple proof is seen in the study of the Creeds of Christendom. The denominations that believe in salvation by works, religious ceremony, or ritual have no place in their confessions for the doctrine of Election. But those who believe in salvation by grace, apart from human merit, have not failed to include the blessed doctrine of election in their written Creeds or Confessions....we believe in salvation by Sovereign Grace....No one will be clearly convinced, as he ought to be, that our salvation flows from the Fountain of Free Mercy until he is acquainted with God's Sovereign, Unconditional, Electing Love. Ignorance of this great biblical truth detracts from divine glory and di-

---

[53] Charles Rosson, "Are you one of God's elect people?" (n.d.); included with permission from the author.

minishes true humility. On the other hand an understanding of Election honors God and humbles man. Therefore, a true biblical view of Election brings Praise, Reverence, Admiration and Worship to God; and brings humility, diligence, consolation and comfort to believers.[54]

(3) It *is* pro-gospel, evangelism and missions. The gospel is the means by which God accomplishes election's purpose. It gives the foundation for missions and evangelism. Election is the very assurance that we will be successful in our witness for Christ. While we do not know who the elect are, we know they are there and will come in God's time through our compassionate and sincere efforts in presenting the gospel (Isaiah 55:11; John 10:27; 6:37, 45;17:20, 21; Acts 15:14; 16:14; 18:27; 2 Timothy 2:9, 10; John 6:37; 17:20,21; 2 Timothy 2:10; Isaiah 55:11; 2 Peter 3:9, 15). "Faith comes from hearing the message, and the message is heard through the Word of Christ" (Romans 10:17).

God uses His Word and gospel witnesses to broadcast His message across the world. No one is ever saved without hearing the gospel. When William Carey, the father of the modern missionary movement, was seeking support in his mission efforts, there was an individual that responded with this objection, "Young man, if God wants to save the heathen, He will do so without your help or mine." This type response was common in those days. Carey, himself a strong Calvinist, was not a hyper-Calvinist and obviously did much to promote world missions. He understood what every Christian should know, that God uses His Word and gospel witnesses to win the lost. God has called us to go to the ends of the earth with the gospel and preach it to every creature (Matthew 28:18–20 2 Thessalonians 2:14; Ephesians 1:5, 13; 2 Timothy 2:10; 1 Peter 1:2). Salvation comes through the redemption of Christ, applied by the Spirit by means of the gospel.

Election does not discourage sinners, but encourages them to come to Christ, who, in turn, welcomes them (Revelation 22:17). Election never closes the door but opens it: "Come, all you who are thirsty, come to the waters; and you who have no money, come, buy and eat! Come, buy wine and milk without money and without cost" (Isaiah 55:1).

Remember, Southern Baptists' great heart for missions was "born and bred" in the midst of strong belief in the doctrines of grace. In no way did our founding fathers see election as a hindrance to evangelism and church growth.

---

[54] Reisinger, *Biblical Doctrine of Election*, 19.

(4) It *is* an encouragement to holiness. It never discourages righteousness and holiness. As a matter of fact, it demands that they be present before full assurance of salvation can be received. True electing grace is not present where there is no holiness. He chose us to be holy and blameless in His sight (Ephesians 1:4). People often argue that if they believed in election, they would not have to repent or be holy because "what will be, will be." Nothing could be further from the truth.

Paul confirmed the election of the Thessalonian Christians because the gospel came to them not simply in words, but also with power, with the Holy Spirit and with deep conviction. These people also were models to all believers. Their faith was known everywhere. They turned from idols to serve the living and true God. Thus they proved they were God's elect. The elect are the ones that repent, believe and maintain good works. These graces, which God gives, are not the cause but the evidence of election. The man who does not pray or repent of his sins or trust in the Person and work of Christ or does not engage in good works has no right to claim that he is one of God's elect (1 Thessalonians 1:3–10; 2 Peter 1:5–10; Philippians 2:12,13; Luke 18:7).

(5) It *is* an encouragement to human responsibility. The false notion that Calvinism discourages responsibility is one of the more common objections to election. Nowhere in the Bible is there even a hint of this. True Calvinism does not promote irresponsibility. Men are responsible and accountable for all they do and say (Romans 14:12; Matthew 12:36–37). We are responsible to repent and believe the gospel (Mark 1:15). We must obey the Ten Commandments and the greatest of all the Commandments (Exodus 20; Romans 2:17–27; Mark 12:28–31). We are responsible to obey all the light God may be pleased to give us. All have some revealed light by which we will be held accountable. These are the light of conscience (Romans 2:15) and the light of nature (Romans 1:19–20), as well as the greater revelation of the law and the gospel.

It must be made clear that just because man is incapable (unwilling) of fulfilling God's requirements, he is not exempt from responsibility. Man's inability to do good because of his stubborn, depraved will does not let him "off the hook" any more than Satan's inability to do righteousness excuses him from eternal destruction.

There are many criminals who say they can't help themselves when it comes to murder, theft, arson, rape, etc. Does their inability excuse them? Of course not. The law is held up before every man as the righteous standard to obey. Nothing but chaos would result if exceptions were made on the basis of inability or unwillingness to obey. We are not excused because we "can't help ourselves." We are most definitely responsible creatures and will be held accountable for all our thoughts, words and deeds (Romans 14:12; Matthew 12:36–37).

(6) It *is* God's sovereign choice. God is the initiator of salvation (Jonah 2:9) and according to His own pleasure elected persons unto salvation before the creation of the world.

The Greek word *eklego* is used in Ephesians 1:4 for *chose*. It is in the aorist tense and the middle voice, indicating God's total independence in election. The verb is reflexive signifying that God not only chose without any outside influence but for Himself. He did it completely in and of Himself, thus ruling out any possibility of merit or influence on man's part.

We love Him because He first loved us (1 John 4:19). Our Lord said, "You did not choose me, but I chose you and appointed you to go and bear fruit-fruit that will last" (John 15:16). It was not on the grounds of any goodness in the sinner. If so, no one would have been elected. Remember, righteousness is not the cause of election but its results. "This is love: not that we loved God, but that he loved us and sent his Son as an atoning sacrifice for our sins" (1 John 4:10).

What an unspeakable debt of love we owe to our sovereign God for His electing grace. All glory goes to Him! When we ponder the true nature of divine election, we are compelled to say with the psalmist, "Not to us, O Lord, not to us but to your name be the glory, because of your love and faithfulness" (Psalm 115:1).

I I

For Whom Did Christ Die?

In my early Christian experience, I took for granted that Jesus' death on the cross paid the full sin debt for every individual that has ever lived, even those who would never receive Him. Nothing else ever occurred to me. I believed and preached the typical Arminian view of the atonement. If someone had told me during those years that Jesus' death on the cross was effectual only for the elect, I would have written him off as heretical. Little did I know that hidden (to me) in the Scriptures was the very real and accurate teaching that indeed affirms that Christ's blood atoned for the sins of the elect only.

This is probably the hardest point in Calvinism for most to accept. When I first began to study it and ask others what they thought, I saw immediately that it elicits in many a very negative response. People become angry and defensive. Often, with more emotion than discernment, the retort is, "Do you mean to tell me that Jesus didn't die for everyone? Have you never read John 3:16?" It is very hard to get past this point. But once you do, the Scripture is clear. As we study this together, I ask you to lay aside your prejudices and emotional responses. Let's objectively look at the Scriptures.

There are two basic views among evangelicals pertaining to the extent of the atonement, answering the question, "For whom did Christ die?"

> First, the Universal View (Christ died for all): "Christ's redeeming work made it possible for everyone to be saved but did not actually secure salvation for anyone. Although Christ died for all men and for every man, only those who believe in Him are saved. His death enabled God to pardon sinners on the condition that they believe, but it did not actually put away anyone's sins. Christ's redemption becomes effective only if man chooses to accept it."

Second, the Limited or Particular View (Christ died for His chosen people only): "Christ's redeeming work was intended to save the elect only and actually secured salvation for them. His death was a substitutionary endurance of the penalty of sin in the place of certain specified sinners. In addition to putting away the sins of His people, Christ's redemption secured everything necessary for their salvation, including faith, which unites them to Him. The gift of faith is infallibly applied by the Spirit to all for whom Christ died, thereby guaranteeing their salvation."[55]

A careful analysis of the first view will reveal some serious inconsistencies with Scripture. The second represents accurate biblical doctrine. By comparing and contrasting these two views we will see what they directly teach or indirectly imply.

First Contrast

The first view teaches that the death of Christ rendered all men savable but actually saves no one. Hence, salvation is not guaranteed to anyone because the ultimate factor is man's fickle, sin cursed will. The sinner's eternal destiny is left to his self-centered desires and perverted discernment. Man becomes the master of his fate and captain of his soul. This inevitably elevates man and gives him far more credit than he deserves. It gives him reason to boast. But remember, in God's salvation, there is no room for boasting (Ephesians 2:9).

The second view declares that we have a guaranteed salvation in Christ. Christ, by His death, actually became a substitute for and saved His people. He came for this purpose. The sin debt has been removed and paid in full for the ones for whom Christ died.

> As far as the east is from the west, so far has he removed our transgressions from us (Psalm 103:12).

> ...she will bear a son, and you shall call his name Jesus, for he will save his people from their sins (Matthew 1:21).

> Just as the Son of Man did not come to be served, but to serve, and to give his life as a ransom for many (Matthew 20:28).

[55] *To Whom He Wills* (Nundah, Queensland: Reformed Literature Society, n.d.), 16.

For the Son of man came to seek and to save that which was lost (Luke 19:10).

All that the Father gives me will come to me, and whoever comes to me I will never drive away (John 6:37).

No one can come to me unless the Father who sent me draws him, and I will raise him up at the last day. It is written in the Prophets: They will all be taught by God. Everyone who listens to the Father and learns from him comes to me (John 6:44–45).

He went on to say, "This is why I told you that no one can come to me unless the Father has enabled him" (John 6:65).

I have other sheep that are not of this sheep pen. I must bring them also. They too will listen to my voice, and there shall be one flock and one shepherd (John 10:16).

For you granted him authority over all people that he might give eternal life to all those you have given him (John 17:2).

The promise is for you and your children and for all who are far off— for all whom the Lord our God will call (Acts 2:39).

When the Gentiles heard this, they were glad and honored the Word of the Lord; and all who were appointed for eternal life believed (Acts 13:48).

Therefore, the promise comes by faith, so that it may be by grace and may be guaranteed to all Abraham's offspring—not only to those who are of the law but also to those who are of the faith of Abraham. He is the father of us all (Romans 4:16).

Since we have now been justified by his blood, how much more shall we be saved from God's wrath through him! For if, when we were God's enemies, we were reconciled to him through the death of his Son, how much more, having been reconciled, shall we be saved through his life! (Romans 5:9, 10).

 Consequently, just as the result of one trespass was condemnation for all men, so also the result of one act of righteousness was justification that brings life for all men. For just as through the disobedience of the one man the many were made sinners, so also through the obedience of the one man the many will be made righteous (Romans 5:18–19).

Yet, before the twins were born or had done anything good or bad— in order that God's purpose in election might stand (Romans 9:11).

For our sake he (God) made him (Christ) to be sin who knew no sin, so that in him we might become the righteousness of God (2 Corinthians 5:21).

Grace to you and peace from God the Father and our Lord Jesus Christ, who gave himself for our sins to deliver us from the present evil age, according to the will of our God and Father (Galatians 1:3–4).

Christ redeemed us from the curse of the law by becoming a curse for us, for it is written: "Cursed is everyone who is hung on a tree" (Galatians 3:13).

And in this one body to reconcile both of them to God through the cross, by which he put to death their hostility (Ephesians 2:16).

Once you were alienated from God and were enemies in your minds because of your evil behavior. But now he has reconciled you by Christ's physical body through death to present you holy in his sight, without blemish and free from accusation (Colossians 1:21–22).

So Christ was sacrificed once to take away the sins of many people; and he will appear a second time, not to bear sin, but to bring salvation to those who are waiting for him (Hebrews 9:28).

The saying is sure and worthy of full acceptance, that Christ Jesus came into the world to save sinners. And I am the foremost of sinners (1 Timothy 1:15).

Then Christ would have had to suffer many times since the creation of the world. But now he has appeared once for all at the end of the ages to do away with sin by the sacrifice of himself (Hebrews 9:26).

He himself bore our sins in his body on the tree, so that we might die to sins and live for righteousness; by his wounds you have been healed (1 Peter 2:24).

For Christ died for sins once for all, the righteous for the unrighteous, to bring you to God. He was put to death in the body but made alive by the Spirit (1 Peter 3:18).

Second Contrast

The first view teaches that Christ's death gives all men a *chance* but actually secured salvation for no one. It resembles gambling. Barring any accident, bad luck, misfortune, or deprivation, *chances* are the sinner will be saved. If things work in his favor, maybe he'll have a seeking heart. If such *chancy* things don't happen, such as the preacher having a flat tire on his way to preach, or the disobedient missionary failing to share the gospel, or bad weather and other distractions just before the invitation is given at the stadium crusade, perhaps sinners will be saved.

Salvation is not by *chance* but by electing grace (Ephesians 2:8–9). Neither this universe nor the salvation or condemnation of sinners are left to luck or caprice. God's providence embraces all things and will infallibly order all things in favor of the elect sinner's salvation. God will move heaven and earth to save even one of His lost sheep (Luke 15:1–7). If one of God's elect is on a remote island or deep in the heart of a jungle where there is no gospel witness, God will see to it that a copy of the Scriptures, or a tract, or some type of gospel witness gets to him as the means to his salvation.

Third Contrast

According to the first view, something is required from the sinner for Christ's death to be "appropriated" or "completed".

The God-hating, Christ-rejecting, Holy Spirit-resisting sinner must cooperate with God to be saved. In essence it says that God cannot save unless men *let* Him. God's will and purposes depend upon man's choice. God's hands are tied. He can't act until man acts. This makes salvation depend on man and not God and creates another form of works salvation. What a poor, pitiful, pathetic picture of God! How dishonoring to our thrice holy, omnipotent, omnipresent, omniscient Lord.

The story is told of a preacher who went to the Kentucky mountains to conduct a revival among some coal miners. He preached for several days with no response. On his last night, in a fit of righteous indignation, he said to the congregation, "God is going to judge you because you won't let Him save you!" In response, an old miner in the back of the church got up and said, "I disagree with you preacher! You just got through telling us that we're not saved because we won't 'let' God save us. Well, if He tries to judge us, we won't *let* Him!"

People argue, "God respects our free choices. He won't force His will on anyone. We're not puppets. Man is made in the image of God and He lets man decide his own eternal destiny." If God leaves man to his *free will*, his sin loving nature and depraved desires will always cause him to *freely* reject Christ.

What about Saul of Tarsus? His conversion stands as a prime example of God's sovereignty in salvation and a puzzle to the Arminians. The resurrected Christ appeared to him on the Damascus Road and arrested his attention and captured his heart. If there ever was a self-righteous, proud Christ-resister, it was Saul. If this Jesus hater had had his way, the name of Jesus would have been completely erased from the human scene. If Jesus had waited for Saul to freely choose to be converted, He would have waited eternally. Why doesn't the Lord intervene in a similar way in the lives of everyone, if indeed He desires to save everyone? Why doesn't He overwhelm everyone with His mighty power? Is it because we won't let Him? Hardly! God can do anything He wants without concern for man's resistance. God can and will save anyone He has set His love upon, regardless of how stubborn or supposedly unreachable he or she seemed to have been.

We must be careful at this point to make clear that God never forces people to be saved. He sovereignly works in their hearts prior to conversion to give a blessed willingness to come.

Upon careful thought, if necessary, I *want* God to "violate" my "free will." I would go head-long into hell if He never "interfered" in my life. I am forever glad that He loved and pursued me in my sin. He gently, lovingly turned me around and caused me to want Christ more than anything else. This is amazing grace.

Salvation is by the merits of *Christ alone*, plus nothing from man. Christ's work on the cross did more than make people savable, redeemable, reconcilable and justifiable. He has and will actually save, redeem, reconcile and justify all that He has intended from eternity.

Man's salvation depends upon God's choice. It is His eternal, unalterable decree and determinate council that decides who will be saved. If Christ died for every individual, then isn't God inconsistent in not providing every person with the opportunity to hear the gospel and respond? Could God be so haphazard as to provide salvation for every individual and then not see to it that each one is given opportunity to hear and believe? Did God purpose to purchase redemption for every individual and then fail to make sure that each hears the gospel, which is the means of obtaining that which was purchased for them? In this did God provide the end but not the means to that end?

Paul makes it clear in Romans 1:18–25 that all men are without excuse, whether they hear the gospel or not. All men have some knowledge of God. However, this knowledge is not saving knowledge. Rather, it is knowledge that renders all men speechless before God and without excuse at the final judgment.

Every individual is part of the condemned race of Adam. We've all sinned in him (Romans 5:12). God is perfectly just in allowing all of us to go on in our sin. He is not obligated to save anyone. He was completely just in not providing a way of salvation for the fallen angels. It is only by His unmerited grace and mercy that any human being can be saved.

Christ tells us that it is our responsibility as the Church to fulfill the Great Commission (Matthew 28:19–20). Paul puts it like this,

> For, everyone who calls on the name of the Lord will be saved. How, then, can they call on the one they have not believed in? And how can they believe in the one of whom they have not heard? And how can they hear without someone preaching to them (Romans 10:13,14)?

Our responsibility is to take the gospel to everyone. However, those who never hear and never believe are not treated unjustly when they are judged because they are without excuse in the first place.

Fourth Contrast

According to the first view, Christ died for multitudes *in vain*. This includes even those who had died and were consigned to hell prior to Jesus' death, not to mention the ones who have rejected Christ since then. How can this be? According to this, Jesus died for Old and New Testament unbelievers, such as Esau, Pharaoh, Jezebel, Judas, Herod, etc. Also, it says that Jesus paid the sin debt for all unbelievers throughout history, including Hitler, Stalin and all who are in hell at this very moment. Jesus tried and failed! His mission was unsuccessful.

Before you entertain such a thought, carefully examine these verses:

> I am the good shepherd. The good shepherd lays down his life for the sheep (John 10:11).

> Just as the Father knows me and I know the Father—and I lay down my life for the sheep. I have other sheep that are not of this sheep pen. I must bring them also. They too will listen to my voice, and there shall be one flock and one shepherd (John 10:15,16).

Notice that the Good Shepherd lays down His life for the sheep, not every individual who ever lived.

> But you do not believe because you are not my sheep. My sheep listen to my voice; I know them, and they follow me. I give them eternal life, and they shall never perish; no one can snatch them out of my hand (John 10:26–28).

The sheep are not those who merely think about following Christ but those who actually hear His voice and follow Him. They are kept eternally by Him:

> I have revealed you to those whom you gave me out of the world. They were yours; you gave them to me and they have obeyed your word (John 17:6).

The Father gave Christ a select number of people, not everyone. Who are they? How can we know if we are His sheep? According to this verse, they are only those who obey His Word. If we don't obey, there is no way to have sound biblical assurance.

> I pray for them. I am not praying for the world, but for those you have given me, for they are yours (John 17:9).

If Jesus prayed for the whole world, then the world would be saved. His intercession is exclusively for those the Father gave Him. Isaiah clearly understood the purpose of the atonement,

> Yet it was the Lord's will to crush him and cause him to suffer, and though the Lord makes his life a guilt offering, he will see his offspring and prolong his days, and the will of the Lord will prosper in his hand. After the suffering of his soul, he will see the light of life and be satisfied by his knowledge my righteous servant will justify many, and he will bear their iniquities. Therefore I will give him a portion among the great, and he will divide the spoils with the strong, because he poured out his life unto death, and was numbered with the transgressors. For he bore the sin of many, and made intercession for the transgressors (Isaiah 53:10–12).

The "many" here is obviously believers. Bearing the sins of many was what His mission required and He accomplished it. Gabriel's announcement to Joseph concerning Jesus' birth emphasizes our Lord's mission. "She will give birth to a son, and you are to give him the name Jesus, because he will save his people from their sins" (Matthew 1:21).

He will save only His people. In Paul's writings to the Corinthian church we find these words, "For as in Adam all die, so in Christ all will be made alive" (1 Corinthians 15:22). The "all" who will be made alive cannot possibly mean everyone who ever lived. It is only those who are brought to life by Christ's regenerating power. The first "all "in this verse includes every person who has ever lived—all who are in Adam; the second "all" includes only the elect—all who are in Christ.

Are we to believe God's plans are unsuccessful? Can God fail? Absolutely not! None of the blood that Jesus shed on the cross was in vain. He accomplished the work He set out to do. If you are in doubt then consider the following verses:

> The Son is the radiance of God's glory and the exact representation of his being, sustaining all things by his powerful word. After he had provided purification for sins, he sat down at the right hand of the Majesty in heaven (Hebrews 1:3).

> Then Christ would have had to suffer many times since the creation of the world. But now he has appeared once for all at the end of the ages to do away with sin by the sacrifice of himself....So Christ was sacrificed once to take away the sins of many people; and he will appear a second time, not to bear sin, but to bring salvation to those who are waiting for him (Hebrews 9:26,28).

> But we ought always to thank God for you, brothers loved by the Lord, because from the beginning God chose you to be saved through the sanctifying work of the Spirit and through belief in the truth. He called you to this through our gospel, that you might share in the glory of our Lord Jesus Christ (2 Thessalonians 2:13–14).

> He saved us, not because of righteous things we had done, but because of his mercy. He saved us through the washing of rebirth and renewal by the Holy Spirit (Titus 3:5).

> For even the Son of Man did not come to be served, but to serve, and to give his life as a ransom for many (Mark 10:45).

> He who did not spare his own Son, but gave him up for us all—how will he not also, along with him, graciously give us all things? Who

will bring any charge against those whom God has chosen? It is God who justifies. Who is he that condemns? Christ Jesus, who died—more than that, who was raised to life—is at the right hand of God and is also interceding for us (Romans 8:32–34).

Fifth Contrast

According to the first view, God's love is temporary with some. Though He loves all men equally today (so says the Arminians), He will cast some, whom He loves or once loved, into hell someday. Is God's love fickle? According to Romans 8:28–39 it is only the foreknown, called, predestined, justified and glorified who will never be separated from God's love. The Arminian view, if carried to its logical conclusion, makes no sense.

Yes, there is a sense in which God loves all men. The cross was displayed for all to see (John 3:16, 12:32). His benevolent goodness and common grace reaches to all people everywhere (Matthew 5:45). Our Lord certainly demonstrated love for all kinds of people as He taught us to do in the parable of the Good Samaritan (Luke 10:25–37). He would not have taught us to practice the Golden Rule had He not done so (Matthew 7:12). He fulfilled the law in every way, including perfect obedience to the second greatest commandment, "love your neighbor as yourself" (Matthew 22:38). However, there is a particular love the Father has for His "dearly loved" (Colossians 3:12). There is a special and exclusive love He has for His elect (Ephesians 1:4–5).

Sixth Contrast

If we follow the first view, God's justice is corrupt because He punished some people eternally in hell for sins Christ *already paid for on the cross*. This is a big, big problem! How do you explain judgment and hell if sins are paid for twice, once by Christ and again by the Christ rejecting sinner in hell? Why doesn't everyone go to heaven if Christ actually paid the sin debt for all?

In a court of law, a person may stand trial and be found guilty for a crime. When he is sentenced and pays his debt to society, he cannot be tried again for the same crime. Double jeopardy is not legal. If our system of justice, imperfect as it is, will not permit this, how could God? His justice is perfect. God is not capable of injustice; therefore, He cannot be guilty of what some have called "Cosmic Double Jeopardy." Either Christ paid the sin debt in full, thus liberating His chosen ones, or the Christ-rejecting sinner pays his own sin debt in hell. It cannot be both.

The typical reply to this is that the sinner's unbelief causes him to go to hell and pay for his sins. But, isn't unbelief a sin? Yes! Didn't Jesus pay for the sin of unbelief on the cross? Yes! Why then must this sin, more than any other, keep anyone out of heaven?

C.H. Spurgeon gives the following splendid explanation:

> Now you are aware that there are different theories of redemption. All Christians hold that Christ came to redeem, but all Christians do not teach the same redemption. We differ as to the nature of atonement and as to the design of redemption. For instance, the Arminian holds that Christ, when He died, did not die with an intent to save any particular person; and they teach that Christ's death does not, in itself, secure beyond doubt the salvation of any one living. They believe that Christ died to make the salvation of all men possible or that by the doing of something else, any man who pleases may attain unto eternal life; consequently, they are obliged to hold that if man's will would not give way and voluntarily surrender to grace, then Christ's atonement would be unavailing. They hold that there was no particularity and specialty in the death of Christ. Christ died, according to them, as much for Judas in hell as for Peter who mounted to Heaven. They believe that for those who are consigned to eternal fire there was as true and eternal redemption made for them as for those who now stand before the Most High. WE BELIEVE NO SUCH THING. We believe that Christ, when He died, had an object in view; and that object will most assuredly and beyond a doubt be accomplished. We measure the design of Christ's death by the effect of it. If anyone asks us, "What did Christ design by His death?" We answer that question by asking him another, "What has Christ done or what will He do by His death?" For we declare that the measure of the effect of Christ's love is the measure of the design of it. We cannot so belie our reason as to think that the intention of the Almighty God could be frustrated or that the design of so great a thing as the atonement can, by any way whatever, be missed. We hold (we are not afraid to say what we believe) that Christ came into the world with the intention of saving a "multitude which no man can number;" and we believe, as a result of this, that every person for whom He died must, beyond a shadow of a doubt, be cleansed from sin and stand washed in the blood before the Father's throne.[56]

[56] C. H. Spurgeon quoted in J. I. Packer, *Evangelism and the Sovereignty of God* (Downers Grove, IL: InterVarsity, 1961), "Introductory Essay," 4.

Contrary to popular opinion, the Universal Atonement view is really the one that limits the atonement. Consider another powerful argument by Spurgeon,

> We are often told that we limit the atonement of Christ, because we say that Christ has not made a satisfaction for all men, or all men would be saved. Now, our reply to this is, that, on the other hand, our opponents limit it: we do not. The Arminians say, Christ died for all men. Ask them what they mean by it. Did Christ die so as to secure the salvation of all men? They say, "No, certainly not." We ask them the next question—Did Christ die so as to secure the salvation of any man in particular? They answer "No." They are obliged to admit this, if they are consistent. They say, "No. Christ has died that any man may be saved if"—and then follow certain conditions of salvation. Now, who is it that limits the death of Christ? Why, you. You say that Christ did not die so as infallibly to secure the salvation of anybody. We beg your pardon, when you say we limit Christ's death; we say, "No, my dear sir, it is you that do it." We say Christ so died that he infallibly secured the salvation of a multitude that no man can number, who through Christ's death not only may be saved, but are saved and cannot by any possibility run the hazard of being anything but saved. You are welcome to your atonement: you may keep it. We will never renounce ours for the sake of it.[57]

Follow the logic of John Owen, considered to be the greatest of all the Puritan theologians, about the extent of the atonement. It is called "Owen's Vice,"

"For Whom Did Christ Die?"

"The Father imposed His wrath due unto, and the Son underwent punishment for, either:

1. All the sins of all men.
2. All the sins of some men, or
3. Some of the sins of all men.

In which case it may be said:

a. That if the last be true, all men have some sins to answer for, and so none are saved.

[57] Ibid.

b. That, if the second be true, then Christ, in their stead suffered for all the sins of all the elect in the whole world, and this is the truth.

c. But if the first be the case, why are not all men free from the punishment due unto their sins?

> You answer, because of unbelief. I ask, is this unbelief a sin, or is it not? If it be, then Christ suffered the punishment due unto it, or He did not. If He did, why must that hinder them more than their other sins for which He died? If He did not, He did not die for all their sins!"[58]

There is a sense in which the death of Christ is universally beneficial to all men or that He died for all without exception:

1. It is universally adequate to save any and all who come to Christ because He alone can save and is the only hope for mankind (Acts 4:12).

2. It is universally sufficient for all men with regard to its power, efficiency, dignity and value. If there were ten billion worlds of sinners, ONE DROP of Christ's precious blood is infinitely more than enough to save them all if God had so designed (John 3:16 and Acts 20:28).

3. It is universally benevolent to all because if it were not for the Lamb slain, all of us would perish (1 Timothy 4:10; 2 Peter 2:1).

4. It is universally gracious to all because all blessings flow from Calvary. While all men are not given God's saving grace, we all are given common grace (Acts 17:24–31 and Matthew 5:45).

---

[58] John Owen, "For Whom Did Christ Die?" (Queensland, Australia: Covenanter Press).

12

The Effectual Call

The Bible tells us that God has chosen the preaching of the cross to call sinners to Christ. The cross is considered foolishness to the lost world, but it is the means by which the power of God unto salvation is demonstrated to all who believe (1 Corinthians 1:21; Romans 1:16).

This is why we must obey the Great Commission to go into all the world and preach the gospel (Matthew 28:19–20). It is a free and sincere offer to everyone. This is what has been called the outward or general call (Matthew 22:14). However, it is puzzling to see some who believe and follow this call while others reject it. Why is it foolishness to some and life to others?

The problem lies in human nature, not the human will. No one by nature will savingly believe in Christ. If God left us to ourselves, we would remain lost. Our natural appetite is for the things of this world. "The man without the Spirit does not accept the things that come from the Spirit of God, for they are foolishness to him, and he cannot understand them, because they are spiritually discerned" (1 Corinthians 2:14).

The only way anyone will ever receive Christ is by the effectual or inward call. Because of the regenerating power of the Holy Spirit, people are enabled to hear the gospel in a different way. Once it was foolishness to them and they responded with passive indifference or active rebellion or both, but when the Spirit awakens the heart, the gospel becomes the most precious thing ever heard (Ephesians 2:1–5).

When our hearts are changed through regeneration or the new birth, we willingly repent of sin and put our faith in Christ. God puts a new heart within us through spiritual creation (Ezekiel 36:26; Ephesians 2:10). Jesus' discussion of the new birth in John 3:1–8 teaches that the Spirit first gives life. When life is given, the sinner is enabled to repent and savingly believe

(Acts 5:31; Ephesians 2:8; Philippians 1:29; Psalm 110:3). This is conversion. Resurrection life comes first before repentance, faith and conversion. He raises His elect from spiritual death (Ephesians 2:1–5). It is mysterious in that no one can explain it. It is sovereign in that He moves when, where and upon whom He wills. When this happens, positive response always takes place. Without exception, all of God's chosen will come to Him: "All that the Father gives me will come to me" (John 6:37).

If the question is asked, "What must I do to be born again?", the answer would be, "Nothing!" We are completely passive in regeneration. If the question is asked, "What must I do to be saved?", the answer would be, "Believe in the Lord Jesus, and you will be saved." (Acts 16:31) In conversion we are active.

We are not to assume, as many do, that this means there may be those who really want to be saved but can't be because they may not be one of the elect. Neither are we to think that there may be those who do not want to be saved but are made to be because they are elect. It must always be remembered that ours is a whosoever gospel (Romans 10:13). It is free. Anyone who truly wants to be saved can be. Someone has said that God's favorite word is "come" (Isaiah 55:1; Matthew 11:28).

My point is, no one remains lost or becomes a Christian against his will. The work of the Spirit in regeneration is never to be thought of as coercion. Rather, it makes Christ so attractive that He becomes irresistible. Salvation becomes something we want so much that we cannot turn it down. In much the same way that a starving man cannot resist nourishment when offered, neither can an awakened sinner, who comes to see his wretched condition, resist Christ's free offer of salvation.

John Wesley popularized a concept called prevenient grace. Prevenient means to "come before." It is a term used to clarify how God's grace works beforehand to save sinners. Prevenient grace means that God gives everyone enough grace to cooperate with Christ and be saved. The question may be asked, "Why did you receive Christ?" The answer, "Because I heard the gospel, the Spirit drew me to Christ and I accepted Him." Then the question is asked, "Why doesn't everyone who hears the gospel receive Christ?" The answer, "Because they resisted the Spirit." At first thought, this seems reasonable. Further consideration, however, will reveal a very serious problem. If people have the knowledge, wisdom and willpower to accept Christ when the Spirit draws, then the inevitable questions we must answer are, "Why then doesn't everyone receive Christ, especially those who have heard the gospel many times? What makes the difference?" If one is not careful at this point, pride will likely raise its ugly head. A superiority of knowledge and righteousness are likely to be claimed. It becomes a matter of boasting. The sinner actually "elects" himself. One has to say that election takes place when the sinner believes, not "before the creation of the world" (Ephesians 1:4). The whole matter of salvation finally rests in man and his ability. If this is the case, then Paul should have said in Romans 9:16, "It does, therefore, depend on man's desire or effort, but not on God's mercy." Instead of, "It does not, therefore, depend on man's desire or effort, but on God's mercy."

Prevenient grace is often used to refute irresistible grace. However, the argument thought to silence the Calvinist, turns out to silence the Arminian. Most Arminians will loudly declare that men are dead in trespasses and sins (Ephesians 2:1), yet contradict themselves by saying he is still alive enough to choose Christ.

We owe an enormous debt of gratitude to R.C. Sproul for his brilliance in defending the doctrines of grace. He has the unique ability to explain complicated subjects in a very simple and convincing way. His refutation of the Arminian view of prevenient grace proves my point:

> As the name suggests, prevenient grace is grace that "comes before" something. It is normally defined as a work that God does for everybody. He gives all people enough grace to respond to Jesus. That is, it is enough grace to make it possible for people to choose Christ. Those who cooperate with and assent to this grace are "elect." Those who refuse to cooperate with this grace are lost.
>
> The strength of this view is that it recognizes that fallen man's spiritual condition is severe enough that it requires God's grace to save him. The weakness of the position may be seen in two ways. If this prevenient grace is merely external to man, then it fails in the same manner that the medicine and the life preserver analogies fail. What good is prevenient grace if offered outwardly to spiritually dead creatures?
>
> On the other hand, if prevenient grace refers to something that God does within the heart of fallen man, then we must ask why it is not always effectual. Why is it that some fallen creatures choose to cooperate with prevenient grace and others choose not to? Doesn't everyone get the same amount?
>
> Think of it this way, in personal terms. If you are a Christian you are surely aware of other people who are not Christians. Why is it that you have chosen Christ and they have not? Why did you say yes to prevenient grace while they said no? Was it because you were more righteous than they were? If so, then indeed you have something in which to boast. Was

that greater righteousness something you achieved on your own or was it the gift of God? If it were something you achieved, then at the bottom line your salvation depended on your own righteousness. If the righteousness was a gift, then why didn't God give the same gift to everybody?

Perhaps it wasn't because you were more righteous. Perhaps it was because you are more intelligent. Why are you more intelligent? Because you study more (which really means you are more righteous)? Or are you more intelligent because God gave you a gift of intelligence he withheld from others?

To be sure, most Christians who hold to the prevenient grace view would shrink from such answers. They see the implied arrogance in them. Rather they are more likely to say, "No, I chose Christ because I recognized my desperate need for him."

That certainly sounds more humble. But I must press the question. Why did you recognize your desperate need for Christ while your neighbor didn't? Was it because you were more righteous than your neighbor, or more intelligent?

The $64 question for advocates of prevenient grace is why some people cooperate with it and others don't. How we answer that will reveal how gracious we believe our salvation really is.

The $64,000 question is, "Does the Bible teach such a doctrine of prevenient grace?" If so, where?

We conclude that our salvation is of the Lord. He is the One who regenerates us. Those whom he regenerates come to Christ. Without regeneration no one will ever come to Christ. With regeneration no one will ever reject him. God's saving grace effects what he intends to effect it by.[59]

Occasionally lost people are spoken of as being hungry for the gospel and eager to hear about the things of God. If it is so, then there are at least two explanations. If there is a true thirst for the gospel, the Holy Spirit has providentially prepared hearts beforehand to hear and receive the gospel. Another explanation may be that they are hungry for a "different gospel" (Galatians 1:6) or "a Jesus other than the one we preached or...a different spirit...or a different gospel" (2 Corinthians 11:4). People do not naturally want the true biblical gospel. They have no appetite for it. The Bible portrays natural man as an outlaw, a rebel, running from God.

[59] Reproduced by permission of Tyndale House Publishers. R. C. Sproul, *Chosen By God* (Chicago, IL: Tyndale House Publishers, 1986), 123-125.

The Jesus of the Bible teaches repentance, self-denial and complete obedience to His Lordship (Mark 1:15; Matthew 16:24–25). He is hated by this world, along with His Word and messengers (John 15:18–21). The gospel must not only be presented to the sinner, but a divine work must be accomplished in the heart if anyone is to be saved.

If it only takes clear, persuasive, powerful, Spirit-filled preaching to get people converted, then how do you explain Jesus' preaching? He is the greatest of all preachers, yet they hated Him for what He said and eventually killed Him. Thus we see that it takes more than preaching or other influences of the Spirit to see true conversion take place. This is why the word *effectual* has been used to describe the nature of God's calling to salvation. It means "producing or sufficient to produce a desired effect; fully adequate." God will inevitably do what He sets out to do.

Ponder R.C. Sproul's brilliant, clear and very convincingly comments on John 6:44:

> "No one can come to Me unless the Father who sent Me draws him" (John 6:44). The key word here is draw. What does it mean for the Father to draw people to Christ? I have often heard this text explained to mean that the Father must woo or entice men to Christ. Unless this wooing takes place, no man will come to Christ. However, man has the ability to resist this wooing and to refuse the enticement. The wooing, though it is necessary, is not compelling. In philosophical language that would mean that the drawing of God is a necessary condition but not a sufficient condition to bring men to Christ. In simpler language it means that we cannot come to Christ without the wooing, but the wooing does not guarantee that we will, in fact, come to Christ.
>
> I am persuaded that the above explanation, which is so widespread, is incorrect. It does violence to the text of Scripture, particularly to the biblical meaning of the word draw. The Greek word used here is "*elko.*" Kittel's Theological Dictionary of the New Testament defines it to mean to compel by irresistible superiority. Linguistically and lexicographically, the word means to "compel."
>
> To compel is a much more forceful concept than to woo. To see this more clearly, let us look for a moment at two other passages in the New Testament where the same Greek word is used. In James 2:6 we read: "But you have dishonored the poor man. Do not the rich oppress you and drag you into the courts?" Guess which word in this passage is the same Greek word that elsewhere is translated by the English word "draw." It is the word "drag." Let us now substitute the word "woo" in the text. It would then read: "Do not the rich oppress you and 'woo' you into the courts?"

The same word occurs in Acts 16:19. "But when her masters say that their hope of profit was gone, they seized Paul and Silas and 'dragged' them into the marketplace to the authorities." Again, try substituting the word "woo" for the word "drag." Paul and Silas were not seized and then wooed into the marketplace.[60]

There is a danger of misunderstanding the effectual call. Let it never be falsely assumed that the sinner is to do nothing. While it is true that no one will be saved without the ministry of the Holy Spirit in regeneration, we are not to wait for the Spirit to move us. The Bible is filled with admonitions to seek the Lord (Isaiah 55:6; Jeremiah 29:13). We are commanded to repent and to believe on the Lord Jesus Christ (Acts 17:30; 16:31).

[60] Reproduced by permission of Tyndale House Publishers. Ibid., 69–71.

13

The Eternal Security
Of the Believer

What truth can be more precious than the assurance of our eternal security as children of God? Security is what the world looks for through gaining wealth, insurance, good health, friends, etc. But all these are only temporary. What good is it to gain all the security the world has to offer and then forfeit our own souls (Mark 8:36–37)? Obviously, God's security is the greatest and only kind that will last when everything else fades away.

Few Southern Baptists would argue against the doctrine of the eternal security of the believer. This is one point we all tenaciously claim and would fight to uphold. However, it is at this point that those who oppose the doctrines of grace do not seem to understand how illogical, inconsistent as well as unscriptural they are.

Some preliminary statements are in order before we can gain a proper understanding of this truth. First, it must be settled as to whether an individual has experienced real salvation. If so, there will never be a falling from grace. If not, saving grace was never received in the first place. However, it is unwise for us to give final judgment because only God ultimately knows. Occasionally we will hear someone say they have known people who were saved but fell away. Again, God must be the judge of such cases. The certainty we can always cling to is that salvation, if once obtained, can never be taken away.

Second, what about the passages that seem to teach falling from grace? Careful study will show that no passage teaches against the eternal security of the saints. There have been countless thousands who have outwardly been numbered among God's people and even experienced many of God's blessings. Judas, one of the twelve, for example, apparently had been given the power to cast out demons, to heal the sick, and to raise the dead (Matthew 10:1–4). Jesus plainly spoke of those whom He will judge someday who will claim to have prophesied, cast out demons, and done many wonders in His name. He will declare to them in the end that He never knew them. He knows all, but He only savingly knows those who do His will (Matthew 7:21–23).

The writer of Hebrews speaks of those who have received unusual blessing and, at first reading leaves us wondering if falling from grace is a possibility (Hebrews 6:4–6, 10:26 and 12:17). Careful examination will prove otherwise. He teaches us that great opportunity calls for great responsibility. If one is exposed to such great revelation and then rejects Christ to the point of deliberately and maliciously trampling His blood, then the day of gospel opportunity ends. The judgment for apostasy is God leaving us to ourselves and giving us over to a seared conscience and a hardened heart. One of the ringing messages of Hebrews is the absolute necessity of the perseverance of the saints. It is essential we understand faith that does not hold out to the end is not saving faith. Third, the doctrine of eternal security does not preclude the possibility of sin in the life of the Christian. Positionally we are perfect in Christ (1 Corinthians 1:30) but practically we are far from perfect: "If we claim to be without sin, we deceive ourselves and the truth is not in us" (1 John 1:8).

Fourth, this doctrine is not a license to sin. An oft quoted assumption is, "If I believe this, it gives me license to do what I want." However, when regeneration takes place, our desires change. If God's Spirit is indwelling me, I don't want to do the things that displease God.

Fifth, this truth involves both the perseverance as well as the preservation of the saints. The doctrine of the perseverance of the saints does not maintain that all who profess the Christian faith are certain of heaven. Only those who are born of the Spirit and endowed with living faith persevere to the end. Many who profess to believe fall away, but they do not fall from grace, because they never had it. True believers do yield to temptation, and often fall into grievous sins, but these sins do not cause them to lose their salvation. The *London Baptist Confession of Faith* gives the following statement about this doctrine:

> Those whom God hath accepted in the Beloved, effectually called and sanctified by the Spirit, and given the precious faith of his elect unto can neither totally nor finally fall away from the state of grace: but shall certainly persevere therein to the end, and be eternally saved [17.3].

The parable of the sower (Matthew 13:3–9 and 18–23) shows that some, who supposedly believed, will not endure. Only those who genuinely receive the Word, persevere in faith and bring forth fruit will be saved. Jesus Himself settled the matter of perseverance in Matthew 24:24 when He said, "For false Christs and false prophets will appear and perform great signs and miracles to deceive even the elect—if that were possible." This teaches that the elect cannot be ultimately deceived to the point of being lost again. Also, in Matthew 24:22, "If those days had not been cut short, no one would survive, but for the sake of the elect those days will be shortened." This shows us that God's judgment will be shortened for the elect's sake. The elect will persevere to the end because they are preserved by God. The very nature of saving faith is that it endures. If faith doesn't endure, it never was genuine in the first place. We will stumble and fall but there will be an undying commitment to cling to Christ and press on by faith.

Pillars That Undergird This Truth

There are certain pillars that undergird the truth of eternal security. Consider some of them with me. First, *the purpose of God in salvation.* Salvation is of God: "Salvation comes from the Lord" (Jonah 2:9). If salvation is of the Lord then how can it fail? Is God's purpose conditional? Does it depend on the whimsical decisions and actions of men? Many think so. How can He be God and fail in His purpose? There is only one true God (Isaiah 46:8–10). To say He can is to say He is less than God. He has predestined His elect to salvation: "When the Gentiles heard this, they were glad and honored the Word of the Lord; and all who were appointed for eternal life believed" (Acts 13:48). These were appointed for eternal life. It is clear that these were not appointed because they believed but they believed because they were appointed. The logical question is, when were they appointed? The answer is clear. It was before the foundation of the world: "For he chose us in him before the creation of the world" (Ephesians 1:4).

Second, *the past tense of salvation.* The Christian is justified, called, predestined and glorified.

> And we know that in all things God works for the good of those who love him, who have been called according to his purpose. For those God foreknew he also predestined to be conformed to the likeness of his Son, that he might be the firstborn among many brothers. And

those he predestined, he also called; those he called, he also justified;
those he justified, he also glorified (Romans 8:28–31).

In this text it is important that we see God's eternal perspective of our
salvation. Our salvation is so complete that it is viewed in the past tense.
The elect are foreknown, predestined, called, justified and glorified. In the
mind of God our salvation is already completed. How then can we lose
what God has already planned and purposed before the creation of the
world? How can God lose a battle or fail in His eternal purpose when
He is almighty? God starts, maintains and finishes His purposes. "Being
confident of this, that he who began a good work in you will carry it on
to completion until the day of Christ Jesus" (Philippians 1:6). "For it is
God who works in you to will and to act according to his good purpose"
(Philippians 2:13).

Third, *the providence of God* proves eternal security. Romans 8:28 gives
us a concise definition of providence, "And we know that in all things God
works for the good of those who love him, who have been called according to his purpose." If everything is fitting into a pattern for good, how
can anything destroy my soul? Another great verse on providence is Psalm
57:2, "I cry out to God Most High, to God, who fulfills his purpose for
me." If God cannot fail in His purpose and He fulfills His purpose for me,
how can I not be finally saved?

Take note of the scriptural accuracy of the *London Baptist Confession
of Faith*, especially about providence,

> God, the good Creator of all things, in his infinite power and wisdom,
> doth uphold, direct, dispose, and govern all creatures (Hebrews 1:3; Job
> 38:11; Isaiah 46:10–11; Psalm 13:6), and things from the greatest even
> to the least (Matthew 10:29–31), by his most wise and holy Providence,
> to the end for which they were created, according unto his infallible fore-
> knowledge, and the free and immutable counsel of his own will (Ephe-
> sians 1:11), to the praise of the glory of his wisdom, power, justice, infi-
> nite goodness and mercy.... As the Providence of God doth in general
> reach to all creatures, so after a more special manner it taketh care of his
> Church (1 Timothy 4:10; Amos 9:8–9; Isaiah 43:3–5) [5.1 and 5.7].

This infallible and unshakable providence, of which the believer is a
special part, guarantees security forever.

Fourth, *the present tense of salvation* verifies my eternal preservation. Notice in the following verses that our salvation is in the present

tense, "I tell you the truth, whoever hears my word and believes him who sent me has eternal life and will not be condemned; he has crossed over from death to life" (John 5:24); "For God so loved the world that he gave his one and only Son, that whoever believes in him shall not perish but have eternal life" (John 3:16); "He who has the Son has life; he who does not have the Son of God does not have life" (1 John 5:12). You can't lose something everlasting. If you can, it wasn't everlasting in the first place. If I can be saved and remain that way until I sin it away or the devil wrestles it away from God, then God lied to me. It was only temporal life at best. God cannot lie. If He tells us that we now have (present tense) eternal life and then later takes it away, He was not truthful. Eternal life begins when an individual is saved. God knows all and He upholds the future as well as He upholds today. Why would He give us salvation today, knowing all the time we will lose it later? Is God fickle? If sinful humans believe it is wrong, inconsistent, unfair, deceptive and untrustworthy to give and then take back, how much more does God?

The doctrine of falling from grace is really another form of salvation by works. To believe this, one has to resort to self boasting, self righteousness and self dependence. How can those who believe it get through even one hour, much less a day or a week with any assurance? What despair, frustration and misery must accompany such a belief!

Fifth, *the position of God's children* shows us that we are as secure as Christ Himself. The phrases "in Christ" and "Christ in you" are found throughout the New Testament. "Therefore, if anyone is in Christ, he is a new creation; the old has gone, the new has come!" (2 Corinthians 5:17). "To them God has chosen to make known among the Gentiles the glorious riches of this mystery, which is Christ in you, the hope of glory" (Colossians 1:27). We are united with Christ and thus identified with Him. "Because in this world we are like him" (1 John 4:17b). Nothing can destroy that vital union.

Satan can't—"We know that anyone born of God does not continue to sin; the one who was born of God keeps him safe, and the evil one cannot harm him" (1 John 5:18).

Sin can't—"For sin shall not be your master, because you are not under law, but under grace" (Romans 6:14).

Temptation can't—"No temptation has seized you except what is common to man. And God is faithful; he will not let you be tempted beyond what you can bear. But when you are tempted, he will also provide a way out so that you can stand up under it" (1 Corinthians 10:13).

The world can't—"For everyone born of God overcomes the world. This is the victory that has overcome the world, even our faith" (1 John 5:4).

God won't—"All that the Father gives me will come to me, and whoever comes to me I will never drive away" (John 6:37).

We ourselves won't—Once we have been changed, we will not go against our own nature. We are no more able to will to go back into spiritual death than we can will to come into spiritual life. Some say that man can still say no to Christ after believing. Will he if he's in his right mind? God's power to save and keep us goes beyond man's will and inability to know the end from the beginning. God's grace allows for man's ignorance.

For the believer to be lost is for Christ to be lost. We are as secure as Christ Himself. "Therefore, there is now no condemnation for those who are in Christ Jesus"(Romans 8:1). Is Christ eternally secure? Of course! Are we in Christ? Yes! If we are in Him, how can we ever be lost? "You, dear children, are from God and have overcome them, because the one who is in you is greater than the one who is in the world"(1 John 4:4). Paul, in Colossians 3:3, powerfully shows us our position with Christ, in God. "For you died, and your life is now hidden with Christ in God."

The story is told of a young preacher who felt that eternal security was a devil's doctrine. He challenged an older preacher in the community to a public debate on the issue. On a certain night, after much publicity, a large crowd gathered. The young preacher got up and argued eloquently against eternal security. Next, the old preacher got up and simply read Colossians 3:3. He then had three boys to help him carry three barrels to the platform, one small, one medium and one large. He placed the small barrel inside the medium barrel and nailed the lid down. He then took the medium sized barrel, containing the small barrel, and placed it inside the large barrel and nailed the top on. He then challenged anyone present to get to the smallest barrel without first going through the first two. The response was plain. No one could do it. Then he read Colossians 3:3 again. He told the crowd to let the small barrel represent the Christian, the medium barrel to represent Christ, and the largest barrel to represent God the Father. He then said in a very loud and powerful voice, "I challenge anyone present, the devils in hell or any power in heaven or on earth to get to my soul without first going through God the Father and Christ the Son. It can't be done. That's how secure I am." Needless to say, the old preacher convincingly won the debate.

Several years ago, when I was pastor of the East Columbia Baptist Church in Columbia, Mississippi, I had a very good friend named Rodney Cook who was pastor of the East Columbia Church of God. We often discussed our doctrinal differences. Being the honest and thorough Bible student he was, he did a great deal of objective study. He began to preach verse by verse through Ephesians. The further he progressed the more he began to see truths he had never seen before. He became convinced of eternal security and has since become an outstanding Southern Baptist pastor and evangelist. He states that he became a Baptist half way through his study of Ephesians because, for the first time, he saw his position "in Christ."

Sixth, *the protection of God* guarantees our security. Because we are God's property, we can be assured that we are under His protection.

Consider the following statements of God's ownership of His people. "And you are of Christ, and Christ is of God" (1 Corinthians 3:23). "Do you not know that your body is a temple of the Holy Spirit, who is in you, whom you have received from God? You are not your own; you were bought at a price. Therefore honor God with your body" (1 Corinthians 6:19–20).

Does God protect His property? Is He responsible? Of course. Therefore, He protects us. Paul, in 2 Timothy 1:12, gives a resounding note of assurance relative to God's protection of His people, "That is why I am suffering as I am. Yet I am not ashamed, because I know whom I have believed, and am convinced that he is able to guard what I have entrusted to him for that day." The idea is that of depositing our lives into the safekeeping of Christ. Just as we trust the bank to keep our money and investments safe, much more, we can trust our Lord to keep safe the investment of our very souls. What about Jesus' blessed assurance of eternal life for His sheep? "My sheep listen to my voice; I know them, and they follow me. I give them eternal life, and they shall never perish; no one can snatch them out of my hand" (John 10:27–28). Satan's power is great, but God is infinitely greater.

Many think that people are responsible enough to safely control their own destiny. If the Christian's destiny is not safe in his own hands after he is saved, how could it be thought to be safe in his own hands before his conversion?

We are kept by God's power. "Who through faith are shielded by God's power until the coming of the salvation that is ready to be revealed" (1 Peter 1:5). "To him who is able to keep you from falling and to present you before his glorious presence without fault and with great joy" (Jude 24). "The one who calls you is faithful and he will do it" (1 Thessalonians 5:24). If we will go to great lengths in protecting our property through insurance, locks, fences, alarms, police protection, etc., how much more will God protect His property? It is impossible for God to lose anything that He has bought with His own blood (Acts 20:28).

Seventh, *the power of grace* assures us of God's keeping power. We are saved by grace and not works. "For it is by grace you have been saved, through faith—and this not from yourselves, it is the gift of God—not by works, so that no one can boast. For we are God's workmanship, created in Christ Jesus to do good works, which God prepared in advance for us to do" (Ephesians 2:8–10). It is not what we do, it is what He has done. It is not our holding on to Christ but Christ holding on to us. If salvation is works, it is ego-centric. If it is grace, it is Christ-o-centric.

We all know the story of Noah and the Ark. God safely kept Noah and his family inside the Ark for the duration of the flood. Suppose God had told Noah not to live inside the Ark but to put pegs on the sides to hang on to during the flood. Imagine Noah's "blessed assurance" when God informed him that he and his family could be saved if they could hold on. Ridiculous? Yes! But untold thousands who believe in falling from grace believe something equally ridiculous. To imagine that my salvation depends on my holding on is to defy the whole meaning and character of grace.

Eighth, *the priesthood of Christ* overwhelms us with assurance. Christ's sacrifice was perfect.

> And by that will, we have been made holy through the sacrifice of the body of Jesus Christ once for all. Day after day every priest stands and performs his religious duties; again and again he offers the same sacrifices, which can never take away sins. But when this priest had offered for all time one sacrifice for sins, he sat down at the right hand of God. Since that time he waits for his enemies to be made his footstool, because by one sacrifice he has made perfect forever those who are being made holy (Hebrews 10:10–14).

The sanctified (saved) are perfected forever because of the one offering of Christ Himself. He ever lives to intercede.

> "Who is he that condemns? Christ Jesus, who dies—more than that, who was raised to life—is at the right hand of God and is also in-

terceding for us" (Romans 8:34). "Therefore he is able to save completely those who come to God through him, because he always lives
to intercede for them" (Hebrews 7:25). "My dear children, I write this
to you so that you will not sin. But if anybody does sin, we have one
who speaks to the Father in our defense—Jesus Christ, the Righteous
One" (1 John 2:1).

Would Jesus, our heavenly lawyer, ever take a case He couldn't win? Is
He that incompetent? Never! He has never lost a case. Jesus prayed for our
eternal security and God honors His prayers and will answer them.

> "I will remain in the world no longer, but they are still in the world,
> and I am coming to you. Holy Father, protect them by the power of
> your name—the name you gave me—so that they may be one as we
> are one…. My prayer is not that you take them out of the world but
> that you protect them from the evil one…. My prayer is not for them
> alone. I pray also for those who will believe in me through their mes-
> sage" (John 17:11–12,15, 20).

Ninth, *the performance of the Spirit* should free us from the fear of ever
being lost. Both Ephesians 1:13–14 and 4:30 tell us that the Holy Spirit is
God's seal guaranteeing our final delivery someday. Also He is our down
payment, giving us a foretaste of future glory.

> "And you also were included in Christ when you heard the Word of
> truth, the gospel of your salvation. Having believed, you were marked
> in him with a seal, the promised Holy Spirit, who is a deposit guar-
> anteeing our inheritance until the redemption of those who are God's
> possession—to the praise of his glory." "And do not grieve the Holy
> Spirit of God, with whom you were sealed for the day of redemp-
> tion."

Would God make a bad investment? If He knows all (beginning to
end), would He invest His Holy Spirit in you, knowing you would fall
someday? Would God guarantee His salvation for you, give you a down
payment of His Holy Spirit and then renege? Would He tell you He will
deliver you to heaven and then lose His way or run into something unfore-
seen? Do we depend on that kind of God? Does our eternal, sovereign, all-
knowing, all-seeing God do business like that? Absolutely not! The God

of the Bible stands firmly behind everything He promises and by His own authority does what He says.

Tenth, *perseverance in holiness* assures us of eternal salvation. Our Lord has made an everlasting covenant with His people, the stipulations of which are given in Jeremiah 30:33–34. By His transforming power He will put His law in our minds and write them upon our hearts. He will be our God and we will be His people. We will know God in a very personal and intimate relationship. He will forgive our sins and never remember them against us again. According to Jeremiah 32:40, "I will make an everlasting covenant with them: and I will never stop doing good to them, and I will inspire them to fear me, so that they will never turn away me."

Our Lord will never stop doing us good. He will put His fear in our hearts so that we will never turn away. We will persevere to the end, not because of our ability to hold out, but because He puts within us everything we need to persevere.

14

Answers to Objections and Questions

There are many questions that inevitably arise as we ponder all these deep things. While the Calvinistic position is often attacked by various critics for what appears to be irrefutable inconsistencies, their questions and objections can be answered with sound biblical facts. Granted, there are many questions Calvinists cannot answer, but, all things considered, neither can anyone else. One of the things that originally drew me to Calvinism was that it meets all difficulties head-on, answers questions with the most sound, soul-satisfying, biblical answers, and is unafraid to admit it doesn't know everything. Arminians are often short-sighted, naive and shallow in their responses. The very objections they use as their "big guns" to refute their opponents turn out to be inconsistent and problematic. I will seek to answer some of the more common questions and objections.

(1) **What about the passages in which such universal words as "world," "all" and "whosoever" are used? Don't these plainly contradict Calvinism?**

This is one of the foremost objections used to oppose Calvinism. On the surface it seems to be a strong argument in favor of Arminianism. Careful examination will prove otherwise.

First of all, the word "world" in Scripture is used in a number of different ways. A.W. Pink's explanation of this word in his classic book *The Sovereignty of God* is clear and convincing:

THE MEANING OF "KOSMOS" IN JOHN 3:16

The word "kosmos," and its English equivalent "world," is *not* used with a *uniform* significance in the New Testament. Very far from it. It is used in quite a number of *different* ways. Below we will refer to a few passages where this term occurs, suggesting a tentative definition in each case:

1. "Kosmos" is used of the Universe as a whole: Acts 17:24—"God that made *the world* and all things therein, seeing that He is Lord *of heaven and earth*."

2. "Kosmos" is used of the earth: John 13:1; Ephesians 1:4; etc., etc.— "When Jesus knew that His hour was come that He should depart *out of this world* unto the Father, having loved His own which were *in the world* He loved them unto the end." "Depart out of this world" signifies, leave this earth.

    "According as He hath chosen us in Him before *the foundation of the world*." This expression signifies, before the earth was founded—compare Job 38:4 etc.

3. "Kosmos" is used of the world-system: John 12:31 etc. "Now *is the judgment* of this *world*: now shall *the Prince of this world* be cast out"—Compare Matthew 4:8 and 1 John 5:19, R.V.

4. "Kosmos" is used of the whole human race: Romans 3:19, etc.—"Now we know that what things soever the law saith, it saith to them who are under the law: that *every* mouth may be stopped, and *all the world* may become guilty before God."

5. "Kosmos" is used of humanity *minus believers*; John 15:18; Romans 3:6— "If *the world hate* you, ye know that it hated Me before it hated you." Believers do not "hate" Christ, so that "the world" here *must* signify the world of *un*-believers in contrast from believers who love Christ.

    "God forbid: for then how shall God *judge the world*." Here is another passage where "the world" *cannot* mean "you, me, and everybody," for *believers will not* be "judged" by God, see John 5:24. So that here, too, it must be the world of *un*-believers which is in view.

6. "Kosmos" is used of Gentiles in contrast from Jews: Romans 11:12 etc. "Now if the fall of them (Israel) be *the riches of the world*, and the diminishing of them (Israel) *the riches of the Gentiles*; how much more their (Israel's) fullness." Note how the first clause in italics is *defined* by the latter clause placed in italics. Here, again, "the world" *cannot* signify all humanity for it *excludes* Israel!

7. "Kosmos" is used of believers only: John 1:29; 3:16, 17; 6:33; 1 Corinthians 4:9; 2 Corinthians 5:19. We leave our readers to turn to these pas-

sages, asking them to note, carefully, *exactly what is said and predicated of* "the world "in each place.

Thus it will be seen that "kosmos" has at least seven clearly defined *different meanings* in the New Testament....The principal subject of John 3:16 is *Christ as the Gift of God*. The first clause tells us *what* moved God to "give" His only begotten Son, and that was His great "love;" the second clause informs us *for whom* God "gave" His Son, and that is for, "whosoever (or, better, 'every one') believeth;" while that last clause makes known *why* God "gave" His Son (His purpose), and that is, that everyone that believeth "should not perish but have everlasting life."

That "the world" in John 3:16 refers to *the world of believers* (God's elect), in contradistinction from "*the world of the ungodly*" (2 Peter 2:5), is established, unequivocally established, by a comparison of the *other* passages which speak of God's "*love*." "God commandeth His love *toward US*"—the saints, Romans 5:8. "*Whom* the Lord loveth He *chasteneth*"—every son, Hebrews 12:6. "We love Him, because He first loved *US*"—believers, 1 John 4:19. The wicked God "pities" (see Matthew 18:33). Unto the unthankful and evil God is "kind" (see Luke 6:35). The vessels of wrath He endures "with much longsuffering" (see Romans 9:22). But "His own" God "*loves*"![61]

Secondly, the word "all" in Scripture has at least two different meanings. There is one sense in which it means all people without exception or with no limit to whom it refers. For example, "...he[God] commands all people everywhere to repent." (Acts 17:30). In the other sense it means all people without distinction. For instance, let's take 2 Peter 3:9. R.C. Sproul gives the best analysis of this verse that I have ever read:

The Apostle Peter clearly states that God is not willing that any should perish. "The Lord is not slack concerning His promise, as some count slackness, but is longsuffering toward us, not willing that any should perish but that all should come to repentance" (2 Peter 3:9). How can we square this verse with predestination? If it is not the will of God to elect everyone unto salvation, how can the Bible then say that God is not willing that any should perish?

In the first place we must understand that the Bible speaks of the will of God in more than one way. For example, the Bible speaks of what we call God's sovereign efficacious will. The sovereign will of God is that

[61] A. W. Pink, *The Sovereignty of God* (Grand Rapids, MI: Baker, 1930), 253-255.

will by which God brings things to pass with absolute certainty. Nothing can resist the will of God in this sense. By his sovereign will he created the world. The light could not have refused to shine.

The second way in which the Bible speaks of the will of God is with respect to what we call his preceptive will. God's preceptive will refers to his commands, his laws. It is God's will that we do the things he mandates. We are capable of disobeying this will. We do in fact break his commandments. We cannot do it with impunity. We do it without his permission or sanction. Yet we do it. We sin.

A third way the Bible speaks of the will of God has reference to God's disposition, to what is pleasing to him. God does not take delight in the death of the wicked. There is a sense in which the punishment of the wicked does not bring joy to God. He chooses to do it because it is good to punish evil. He delights in the righteousness of his judgment but is "sad" that such righteous judgment must be carried out. It is something like a judge sitting on a bench and sentencing his own son to prison.

Let us apply these three possible definitions to the passage in II Peter. If we take the blanket statement, "God is not willing that any should perish," and apply the sovereign efficacious will to it, the conclusion is obvious. No one will perish. If God sovereignly decrees that no one should perish, and God is God, then certainly no one will ever perish. This would then be a proof text not for Arminianism but for universalism. The text would then prove too much for Arminians.

Suppose we apply the definition of the preceptive will of God to this passage? Then the passage would mean that God does not allow anyone to perish. That is, he forbids the perishing of people. It is against his law. If people then went ahead and perished, God would have to punish them for perishing. His punishment for perishing would be more perishing. But how does one engage in more perishing than perishing? This definition will not work in this passage. It makes no sense.

The third alternative is that God takes no delight in the perishing of people. This squares with what the Bible says elsewhere about God's disposition toward the lost. This definition could fit this passage. Peter may simply be saying here that God takes no delight in the perishing of anyone.

Though the third definition is a possible and attractive one to use in resolving this passage with what the Bible teaches about predestination, there is yet another factor to be considered. The text says more than simply that God is not willing that any should perish. The whole clause is important: "but is longsuffering toward us, not willing that any should perish but that all should come to repentance."

What is the antecedent of any? It is clearly us. Does us refer to all of us humans? Or does it refer to us Christians, the people of God? Peter is fond of speaking of the elect as a special group of people. I think what he is saying here is that God does not will that any of us (the elect) perish. If that is his meaning, then the text would demand the first definition and would be one more strong passage in favor of predestination.

In two different ways the text may easily be harmonized with pre-destination. In no way does it support Arminianism. Its only other possible meaning would be universalism, which would then bring it into conflict with everything else the Bible says against universalism.[62]

Consider Loraine Boettner's exposition of this verse:

Arminians insist that in 2 Peter 3:9 the words "any" and "all" refer to all mankind without exception. But it is important first of all to see to whom those words were addressed. In the first verse of chapter 1, we find that the epistle is addressed not to mankind at large, but to Christians: "...to them that have obtained a like precious faith with us." And in a preceding verse (3:1), Peter had addressed those to whom he was writing as "beloved." And when we look at the verse as a whole, and not merely at the last half, we find that it is not primarily a salvation verse at all, but a second coming verse! It begins by saying that "The Lord is not slacking concerning his promise" [singular]. What promise? Verse 4 tells us: "the promise of his coming." The reference is to His second coming, when He will come for judgment, and the wicked will perish in the lake of fire. The verse has reference to a limited group. It says that the Lord is "longsuffering to usward," His elect, many of whom had not yet been regenerated, and who therefore had not yet come to repentance. Hence we may quite properly read verse 9 as follows: "The Lord is not slack concerning his promise as some count slackness, but is longsuffering *to usward*, not willing that any *of us* should perish, but that all *of us* should come to repentance.[63]

Another verse that gives some difficulty is 1 Timothy 2:4, 6, "...who wants all men to be saved and to come to a knowledge of the truth.... who gave himself as a ransom for all men." In following one of the cardinal principles of biblical interpretation, that of examining the context, we are able to see that the "all" the writer is using in this text refers *not to all men*

---

[62] Reproduced by permission of Tyndale House Publishers. R. C. Sproul, *Chosen By God* (Chicago, IL: Tyndale House Publishers, 1986), 195-197.

[63] Loraine Boettner, *The Reformed Doctrine of Predestination* (Phillipsburg, NJ: Presbyterian and Reformed, 1982), 19-20.

without exception but to all men without distinction or to distinctive groups of people, such as rich and poor, bond and free, Jew and Gentiles.

The Jews were God's chosen people. They were uniquely blessed above every other nation. God sovereignly chose them exclusively to receive the law of God and the gospel. It was through them that Christ came into the world. Because their self righteous pride blinded them to God's missionary message, they became very intolerant of other people and intensely nationalistic. They were not willing to see themselves as a representative people to the entire world. Racial and religious prejudice was extremely hard for them to overcome. Peter's experience in Acts 10–11 with the Roman Centurion Cornelius gives us an idea of the difficulty the Christian Jews had in preaching the gospel to Gentiles.

In our day it is difficult for us to realize the incredible exclusivism that existed among the Jews in those days. We take verses such as Acts 1:8, 11:18, 15:11, 22:15 for granted, not understanding the tremendous struggle they experienced in coming to "realize how true it is that God does not show favoritism but accepts men from every nation who fear him and do what is right" (Acts 10:34–35).

Therefore, the "all men" and "a ransom for all" of 1 Timothy 2:4, 6 speaks of Gentiles as well as Jews, not every human being that has or ever will live on the face of the earth. Paul was simply seeking to correct the false notion that salvation was for the Jews alone. Other texts in which "all" is used in this way are: 1 Timothy 4:10; Titus 2:11; Hebrews 2:9 and John 12:32.

Another way in which "all" is used in a limited sense is in Mark 1:5, "The whole Judean countryside and all the people of Jerusalem went out to him [John the Baptist]. Confessing their sins, they were baptized by him in the Jordan River." It is obvious that this does not speak of every person without exception. We know that John's preaching did not produce repentance in every individual throughout Judea and Jerusalem. Also in Acts 4:21, "…because all the people were praising God for what had happened." This scene in Jerusalem was certainly not of praise from the enemies of Christ.

It is important that we understand "all" the way it is used in 1 Corinthians 15:22, "For as in Adam all die, so in Christ all will be made alive." From the context Paul is speaking on the resurrection of Christ and of the Christian. The "all" in the first part of the verse plainly indicates every person without exception because all die physically and spiritually in Adam. In the second part the "all" refers to a limited number. He speaks only of those in Christ who will be made alive on the day of resurrection at Christ's coming.

In the third place, the word "whosoever" indicates how glorious our gospel is. It is the free and sincere offer of God's gracious salvation to all people everywhere, no matter what race, creed or economic standing. What an unspeakably wonderful promise to a world full of guilty, hell-deserving sinners. If we believe in God's Son, we will never perish but have everlasting life. The "whosoever" gospel invitation is throughout the Bible.

However, the big question we must answer is, why then do people not come to Christ? After all, the gospel is free. The Water of Life flows abundantly for the thirsty soul. The Bread of Life is available for those who long to be nourished by it. Why don't people rush to receive it? The problem is that people are not thirsty or hungry for the gospel. We have a "whosoever will" gospel in a world of "whosoever won'ts." People just don't want to get rid of their self-rule, self-reliance, sinful pleasures and their captivating idols.

The problem is explained in the context of John 3:16. A casual reading of verses 19–20 is very revealing,

> This is the verdict: Light has come into the world, but men loved darkness instead of light because their deeds were evil. Everyone who does evil hates the light, and will not come into the light for fear that his deeds will be exposed.

Men love darkness and run from the light. Jeremiah 13:23 gives an insightful answer, "Can the Ethiopian change his skin or the leopard its spots? Neither can you do good who are accustomed to doing evil." Man is accustomed to doing evil. It's not that he cannot come. God certainly places no barriers in his way. No one can rightfully point a finger of blame at God. The big problem is that man will not come. He is born with a built-in hostility to God. "…the sinful mind is hostile to God. It does not submit to God's law, nor can it do so" (Romans 8:7). However, God graciously continues to hold out His hand of mercy to "whosoever will" (Revelation 22:17). As with Israel, so with us, "All day long I have held out my hands to a disobedient and obstinate people" (Romans 10:21).

(2) What if there is someone who truly wants to be saved but is not one of the elect? Is there any hope for him?

There is no such thing as a person who truly wants to be saved who can't be. The sincere seeker will surely be saved (Jeremiah 29:13). On the other hand, there is no such thing as a man who, in and of himself, ever wants to come to the Savior. His desires must be changed from the inside. This is where God's work of regeneration comes in. God awakens the sinner, transforms him and writes His law upon his heart (Jeremiah 31:33–34). He changes his "wanter" so that he thirsts for the gospel and knows that he will perish without it. Remember, election is a doctrine of grace. It does not shut people out. It is God's glorious plan to let unworthy sinners in. "All that the Father gives me will come to me, and whoever comes to me I will never drive away" (John 6:37).

If you fear that you may not be one of the elect, carefully read what the famous Puritan Joseph Alleine said,

> You begin at the wrong end if you first dispute about your election. Prove your conversion, and then never doubt your election. If you cannot yet prove it, set upon a present and thorough turning. Whatever God's purposes be, which are secret, I am sure His promises are plain. How desperately do rebels argue! "If I am elected I shall be saved, do what I will. If not, I shall be damned, do what I can." Perverse sinner, will you begin where you should end? Is not the Word before you? What saith it? Repent and be converted, that your sins may be blotted out (Acts 3:19). If you mortify the deeds of the body you shall live (Romans 8:13). Believe and be saved (Acts 16:31). What can be plainer? Do not stand still disputing about your election, but set to repenting and believing. Cry to God for converting grace. Revealed things belong to you; in these busy yourself. It is just, as one well said, that they who will not feed on the plain food of the Word should be choked with the bones. Whatever God's purposes may be, I am sure His promises are true. Whatever the decrees of heaven may be, I am sure that if I repent and believe I shall be saved; and that if I do not repent, I shall be damned. Is not this plain ground for you; and will you yet run upon the rocks.[64]

---

[64] Joseph Alleine, *Alarm To The Unconverted* (London: Banner of Truth, 1959), 12.

(3) Doesn't Calvinism greatly hinder and even, in some cases stop
      evangelism and missions? If everything is predestined and
      God has already chosen His people, why try to evangelize?
      Won't those whom God has chosen be saved regardless of our
      efforts? Let's be honest, Calvinism is a drag on evangelism.

First, we are commanded to go into all the world and make disciples of
all nations (Matthew 28:18–20). The very fact that God says to do it is sufficient reason in itself. We disobey God and sin greatly when we don't go.

Second, election is the only hope of success for the gospel witness. It is
God's infallible assurance. Without it, the gospel invitation would go un-
heeded. Instead of being a hindrance to evangelism, it is our primary motivation that thrusts us out into the harvest fields. We know God is going
to save a people from every nation, tribe, people and language (Revelation
7:9). That gives us encouragement. While many turn away and care nothing for the gospel, there is an unnumbered multitude that will respond and
receive Christ. The greatest missionaries in the history of the church have
been people who believed in unconditional election.

Ezekiel had no hope whatsoever of resurrecting the valley of dry
bones. He knew it had to be the work of God alone. He prophesied as God
commanded and the breath of God did a miraculous work (Ezekiel 37). In
the same way, without the life giving Holy Spirit to make our evangelistic
work effectual, we are helpless indeed. Man's sin-hardened nature would
cause us to cease our evangelistic work in deepest despair if we relied on
our own power to persuade men. Our conviction, however, is that when we
prophecy, God will sovereignly breath on the "dry bones" of dead, yet elect,
sinners and make them live.

Third, God has appointed means in the salvation of sinners. It is
by the foolishness of preaching the message of the cross that people are
saved (1 Corinthians 1:18–25). Sandwiched between two of the greatest
chapters in the Bible on the sovereign election of God is Romans 10. It
teaches the responsibility of man in the realm of evangelism.

> "Everyone who calls on the name of the Lord will be saved." How,
> then, can they call on the one they have not believed in? And how
> can they believe in the one of whom they have not heard? And how
> can they hear without someone preaching to them? And how can
> they preach unless they are sent? As it is written, "How beautiful are

the feet of those who bring good news!" ...faith comes from hearing
the message, and the message is heard through the Word of Christ
(Romans 10:13–15 and 17).

God's appointed way to be saved is through Christ (John 14:6). If anyone is ever saved, he must hear and believe the gospel (Acts 4:12). That's
why the gospel must be carried throughout the world.

Also, no one but God knows who the elect are. If there was some way
to know, then we could simply go and preach to them. In our mission work,
we seek to gather the elect. "Therefore I endure everything for the sake of
the elect, that they too may obtain the salvation that is in Christ Jesus, with
eternal glory" (2 Timothy 2:10). The true church is made up of the sheep
only (John 10). Many faulty evangelistic methods bring in goats—unbelievers—and this is part of what is wrong with churches today. Churches
are to be filled with sheep—the elect—not goats. We are absolutely confident that, through the gospel, God will call His sheep into the fold at His
appointed time. We must, at all costs, avoid sub-biblical practices in our
evangelism. As we sow the gospel seeds, God will surely give a harvest. "He
who goes out weeping, carrying seed to sow, will return with songs of joy,
carrying sheaves with him" (Psalm 126:6).

(4) Are only Calvinists true Christians? Do you have to believe the five points to be saved?

No! How unwise and unfair to make such a claim. Arminianism contains some gospel light. God is often pleased to use a little light to lead
many to greater light.

For the purpose of illustration, Calvinism and Arminianism may be
compared to the difference between pure gold and gold ore. There is gold
in the ore but it must be refined. If a choice was given, all would certainly
take the pure gold over the ore. Refining involves the process of skimming
away the dross for the purpose of purification. Obviously the pure gold is
far more valuable.

Similarly, Calvinism represents for us the pure gold of the gospel.
Arminianism represents the ore which contains much foreign material in
the form of free-willism and human merit. This must be cleared away in
order for the complete value of the gospel to be realized. Arminianism
inevitably and eventually drifts further and further into humanism, uni-

versalism, paganism and complete atheism. It is the ongoing task of every Christian generation to remove the dross and insure the purity of the gospel.

Men are by nature Arminian. We naturally want to know we have everything under control, including God. It is extremely difficult for man to accept the fact that he is not the master of his fate nor captain of his soul. That our destiny is absolutely in the hands of the eternal sovereign God of heaven is a fact of Scripture which we all must come to know.

(5) How many of the five points of Calvinism do most Southern Baptists believe today?

Most in our convention would hold to the first and last points of Calvinism, that of total depravity and perseverance of the saints. There is a growing number who believe in unconditional election. The term "Calminianism" has been coined by some to describe the mixture of Calvinism and Arminianism that many embrace.

Today, this historic faith is making a major comeback. In 2006 the *Baptist Press News* published the results of a survey revealing that approximately 10% of Southern Baptist pastors are five-point Calvinists.[65] That may not seem like many, but one does not have to hold to all five points to be a Calvinist. Speaking from a historical stand-point, even those who only believe the first and last points must admit a Calvinistic leaning. Certainly the three and four pointers legitimately belong in the Calvinistic camp. What about the significant number of Calvinistic college and seminary professors, not to mention denominational workers, IMB and NAMB missionaries? There is certainly something to be said about the large numbers of lay-people who hold to these truths. What about the "closet Calvinists" who, for a variety of reasons, have not yet "come out?"

(6) Why are the five points so important?

Dr. Packer has already been quoted as saying that all five points of Calvinism stand or fall together. One cannot consistently believe one without believing all five. If all men are lost in sin, dead spiritually, hostile toward God and will not come to Christ or seek Him that they may have life, then God must supernaturally intervene in order for salvation to occur. Man de-

---

[65] Reported in *Baptist Press News*, September 18, 2006.

serves no credit. God must take the initiative and give saving faith because all man's righteous acts are as filthy rags in God's sight.

When Christ died, the sin debt was paid, not potentially but actually. He really did become a substitute for His people and pay the penalty for their sins. If He were a substitute for those who do not believe, then sin's debt is paid twice, once on the cross by Christ and also by the sinner in hell. That is double jeopardy (the act of putting a person through a second trial for an offense for which he has already been prosecuted and punished) and with God that cannot be. Also, grace must be irresistible if sinful man ever accepts it. Men must be regenerated and effectually or completely drawn all the way to Christ. God must change our stubborn and rebellious hearts in order for us to be willing to come to Christ, else we would never come. Last of all, if it were left up to the individual to keep himself saved, he would certainly fall away. Only God has the power to save us and keep us.

As has already been pointed out, the term "Calvinism" is a nickname for the gospel. Critics have told me to "quit preaching Calvinism and preach the Bible." My answer is obvious. Calvinism is the entire biblical message of grace. From Genesis to Revelation, it is the gospel of God's unmerited loving kindness and tender mercy given to undeserving sinners.

(7) If the doctrines of grace are taught in Scripture, then why don't more people believe them?

I believe there are several reasons:

1. *Divine Illumination*—The spiritual things of God can only be made known by the Holy Spirit. While there are many biblical facts that any person can grasp, the Spirit alone is able to illumine the deep things of God and place them in our hearts.

> The Spirit searches all things, even the deep things of God... In the same way no one knows the thoughts of God except the Spirit of God....We have not received the spirit of the world but the Spirit who is from God, that we may understand what God has freely given us. This is what we speak, not in words taught us by human wisdom but in words taught by the Spirit, expressing spiritual truths in spiritual words (1 Corinthians 2:10–13).

We Calvinists have been accused of setting ourselves up as the spiritually elite. To some we seem arrogant and pompous. God forbid!

May God forgive those of us who have presented this image. We must not take credit for what God has done? "What do you have that you did not receive? And if you did receive it, why do you boast as though you did not?" (1 Corinthians 4:7). I believeif any true Christian will humbly, honestly and openly ask God to reveal these things, He will do so.

2. *Doctrinal Prejudice*—Prejudice is just as real in theological circles as in race, politics, etc. We tend to embrace that which we have been taught by those whom we have admired, be it professors, pastors, parents or other authority figures. We often do not practice the scriptural admonition: "Test everything. Hold on to the good" (1 Thessalonians 5:21). We often think that if some system of belief is okay for certain successful, significant others, it is okay for us. This is obviously good when truth is believed. In many however, there regretfully develops a hardness in an unbiblical system of belief. This hardness can become so ingrained that other views are never seriously and thoroughly considered, even though strong biblical evidence is presented. It is one of the most dangerous traps into which an individual can fall.

    Pride often plays a very significant roll in keeping us in our unbiblical prejudices. Many simply do not want to risk admitting they are wrong. Certain measures are taken in an effort to "save face" or avoid being labeled. For fear of "losing their ministries" there are influential preachers who are not willing to change, even when the truth is obvious. There are none so blind that will not see or so deaf that will not hear. It should be the commitment of every Bible student to change beliefs and practices wherever the Bible says so, regardless of previously held views.

3. *Neglect and Ignorance*—There are many, even in ministry, with years of formal training and experience in Southern Baptist churches and institutions that simply have never been taught the doctrines of grace. It is not unfair or inaccurate to say that many trained seminarians, pastors and even professors have an inadequate understanding. They see no significance to Calvinism in Southern Baptist history.

4. *Carelessness in Exposition of Scripture*—I must confess that my early years of Bible study and sermon preparation left much to be desired. I would often use other men's sermons and rely on their preparation.

As a result, I tended not to study the Scriptures for myself. However, over the years God was pleased to help me overcome this. Through discipline and putting aside my prejudices, I adopted the Berean system of Bible study, "Now the Bereans were of more noble character than the Thessalonians, for they received the message with great eagerness and examined the Scriptures every day to see if what Paul said was true" (Acts 17:11).

Irresponsible Bible study should never be tolerated, no matter how it may disguise itself. "Do your best to present yourself to God as one approved, a workman who does not need to be ashamed and who correctly handles the Word of truth" (2 Timothy 2:15).

5. *Satanic Deception*—If there is anything Satan hates it is truth. He is the father of lies and the master deceiver (John 8:44–47). When the truth arises, he takes all his satanic weapons and fights it with all his might. His diabolical purpose is to destroy truth.

> And even if our gospel is veiled, it is veiled to those who are perishing. The god of this age has blinded the minds of unbelievers, so that they cannot see the light of the gospel of the glory of Christ, who is the image of God (2 Corinthians 4:3–4).

6. *Stubborn, Unfounded, Unwillingness to Believe the Doctrines of Grace*—There are those that will flatly say they don't want to believe the doctrines of grace. They can't disprove them nor do they even try. Yet because these truths are so foreign to what they have always been taught, they stubbornly dismiss them without any kind of fair investigation. One person was quoted as saying, "I just wish these deep complicated things were not in the Bible!" Many Baptists are content to remain in a "business as usual" posture. Golden calves of tradition have stood in the way of many. They question, "Why has all this 'Calvinism stuff' suddenly become so important?"

Many say, "For years we've gotten along fine without these things you're preaching. It upsets people. It's divisive and confusing. If you want to believe it, then keep it to yourself or go preach somewhere else." One of the saddest and most disturbing facts about the majority of Southern Baptists is that we are not grounded in the faith. The average church member, if pressed to defend and articulate his faith, could not do so.

(8)   Why be so insistent in splitting theological hairs? Isn't it true
      that more confusion results when we try to be "nit-picky"
      about theological matters? If the theologians disagree, who
      are we to question them?

When I was a boy, my Dad was a land surveyor. It was his job to lo-
cate and establish land lines and property corners. He used a very delicate
instrument called a transit. Exactness was very important. If the transit was
off only a fraction, then several hundred feet away the land line or corner
may be missed by several feet. It was the job of my brothers and I to use
axes and bush-hooks to cut the line trails. Many times I can remember cut-
ting a trail, only to have to go back and do it again because the transit was
slightly off. We quickly learned the importance of precision.

If you were in need of surgery, you would not want to trust a doctor
who did not appreciate exactness. A pharmacist who does not dispense
medicine with minute detail would not long be trusted. I certainly would
not want to fly in an airplane that was not built by highly skilled techni-
cians who cared about meticulous detail.

Do I make my point? Doctrinal exactness is of utmost importance.
More confusion and doctrinal instability eventually results when we are
not initially insistent on biblical accuracy. Yes, it seems less complicated to
let someone else do our hard study for us. Why not accept what a seminary
trained pastor or famous TV preacher says, and not think for ourselves? Of
course, we should not error on the opposite side and be suspicious of everyone. Nor should we resist being under the authority and in submission to
God-called, Spirit-led leadership. However, we must learn the difference
between discernment and gullibility. It is easy to be swept off our feet by
some dynamic, suave, smooth-talking preacher that may not be biblically
sound. This happens all too often.

It is strange how we all insist on exactness in almost every area of
life except in biblical knowledge. Often we are too willing to settle for
a vague understanding of a very important doctrinal matter. We end up
being tossed to and fro with every wind of strange teaching and never become established in the faith. It may not seem important at the moment,
but error now could result in condemnation later. Yes, theological "hair
splitting" is extremely important. We should insist on it, even at the risk
of being ostracized and accused of fanaticism. Our spiritual and eternal
welfare depend on it.

(9) Is it really true that God foreordained sin? If so, doesn't this make God the author of sin?

Is there anything man ever does that is not tainted by sin, at least to some degree? Think of history. If sin had not been decreed, then all history would be outside God's plan. Virtually everything man has ever done throughout history has been contaminated with sin. Can we honestly say that the fall of Adam, the crucifixion of Christ, all wars, Hitler's Holocaust, abortions, racial violence, uncontrolled crime and the rise and fall of nations have not all, in some way, fit into God's eternal plan (Ephesians 1:11)? If they have not, then we cannot truthfully say that God is sovereign.

The biblical accounts of the selling of Joseph and the crucifixion of Christ are two instances especially taught where everything, including sin, is ordained by God (Genesis 37–50; Acts 2:23; 4:27–28). Joseph's wicked brothers hated him and had nothing good in mind when they sold him into slavery. They meant it for evil but God meant it for good in order to accomplish His divine purpose (Genesis 50:20). The brothers were guilty, not God. Yet God used these events and people to accomplish His will.

The worst sin ever committed was the crucifixion of Christ. It was "with the help of wicked men" that Jesus was put to death. Yet it was also "by God's set purpose and foreknowledge." Here God's infinite wisdom and power are demonstrated in that He used the most heinous sin ever committed to accomplish His most glorious work.

James gives us much insight at this point,

> When tempted, no one should say, "God is tempting me." For God cannot be tempted by evil, nor does he tempt anyone; but each one is tempted when, by his own evil desire, he is dragged away and enticed (James 1:13–14).

This plainly states that God is not sinful or the author of sin. G.I. Williamson in his commentary of the *Westminster Confession of Faith* puts it this way,

> The apparent contradiction has been put this way: (a) God is the author of all that is. (b) Sin is. (c) Yet God is not the author of sin. But the contradiction is only apparent. For God is not the author of all that is although he has decreed all. Satan and his host (of men and angels) are

the "authors" of sin, although God has created them and decreed even their sin without being himself the author of it.[66]

Sin comes from within the heart of man (Mark 7:21–23). Exactly how God is able to work all things, even the sinful acts of men after the purpose of His own will and, yet, not be the instigator of sin or even be capable of sin is not known. It is an unfathomable mystery solved only in the mind of God. I leave you with a verse that has always given me peace on this mysterious subject, "For the Lord is good and his love endures forever; his faithfulness continues through all generations" (Psalm 100:5).

(10) What about the sovereignty of God and the responsibility of man? Isn't there an irreconcilable problem there?

One of the most helpful books I have found on this subject is *Evangelism and The Sovereignty of God* by J.I. Packer. With the concept of an *antinomy* he illustrates the tension we should constantly maintain with the sovereignty of God and the responsibility of man. Webster defines an antinomy as "a contradiction or inconsistency between two apparently reasonable principles or laws." The Bible teaches undeniably the great truth of the absolute sovereignty of God. God is 100% sovereign and man is 100% responsible. Both are equally true. We are to maintain a balanced tension and believe both.

But how can this be? If God has decreed all things and everything is in His preordained plan, then where does man fit in? Is he some sort of puppet or robot? No! The Bible affirms that man makes real choices with real consequences. He is totally responsible and accountable for all he does. The big question is "How do we bring the two together?" There doesn't seem to be a way. This is the antinomy.

By faith we must accept the antinomy and embrace both, teach both, live both and be content with both, even though, in our minds, it may seem illogical. To follow logic in this matter rather that biblical revelation, and go to extremes either way will always eventually lead to error. It is an ever present temptation we should faithfully resist. Keeping balance between the two is the key. This is what the Bible does, therefore, it should be what we do as well. May God enable us to love this antinomy.

[66] G. I. Williamson, *The Westminster Confession of Faith for Study Classes* (Phillipsburg, NJ: Presbyterian and Reformed Publishing, 1964), 50.

In 1859, Basil Manly Jr. framed the founding confession of the Southern Baptist Theological Seminary entitled the *Abstract of Principles*. He was a Calvinist. Article IV on Providence reveals a healthy, theological balance. Manly wrote:

> God from eternity decrees or permits all things that come to pass, and perpetually upholds, directs and governs all creatures and all events; yet so as not in any wise to be author or approver of sin nor to destroy the freewill and responsibility of intelligent creatures.

On August 1, 1858, C.H. Spurgeon, a passionate soul-winner and a five point Calvinist preached a sermon entitled, "Sovereign Grace and Man's Responsibility" in which he said:

> I see in one place, God presiding over all in providence; and yet I see and I cannot help seeing, that man acts as he pleases, and that God has left his actions to his own will, in a great measure. Now, if I were to declare that man was so free to act, that there was no precedence of God over his action, I should be driven very near to Atheism; and if, on the other hand, I declare that God so overrules all things, as that man is not free enough to be responsible, I am driven at once into Antinomianism or fatalism. That God predestines, and that man is responsible, are two things that few can see. They are believed to be inconsistent and contradictory; but they are not. It is just the fault of our weak judgment. Two truths cannot be contradictory to each other. If, then, I find taught in one place that everything is fore-ordained, that is true; and if I find in another place that man is responsible for all his actions, that is true; and it is my folly that leads me to imagine that two truths can ever contradict each other. These two truths, I do not believe, can ever be welded into one upon any human anvil, but one they shall be in eternity: they are two lines that are so nearly parallel, that the mind that shall pursue them farthest, will never discover that they converge; but they do converge, and they will meet somewhere in eternity, close to the throne of God, whence all truth doth spring.[67]

This is not to say that we are to commit intellectual suicide and throw reason and logic out the window to be a Calvinist. Our intellect is to be in

---

[67] C. H. Spurgeon, *The New Park Street Pulpit*, Vol. 4. (Grand Rapids, MI: Baker Books, 1994), 337.

submission to His Word. Simply put, we are to bow to our blessed Lord as our final authority and leave the harmonizing to Him.

(11) Does Calvinism teach that babies and mentally handicapped people go to hell? What about the phrase in the *Philadelphia Confession of Faith* that speaks of "elect infants?" Does this mean there are "non-elect infants?"

It must first be understood that the Bible only gives two direct statements on this subject. One is where Jesus, in Luke 18:15–16 (and parallel passages), says children, even tiny infants are members of the Kingdom of God. The other is in 2 Samuel 12:23 where King David indicated that his dead baby was in heaven. Other than these, we can only gather inferences. However, these reasons, as we will see, proves the point sufficiently.

Consider the following statement from paragraph 3 in chapter 10, "Of Effectual Calling," in the *London Baptist Confession of Faith*:

> Elect infants dying in infancy, are regenerated and saved by Christ through the Spirit, who worketh when and where, and how he pleaseth; so also are all other elect persons, who are incapable of being outwardly called by the ministry of the Word.

A.A. Hodge in his commentary of the *Westminster Confession of Faith* states that those who formed the confession never "intended to suggest that there are any infants not elect."[68] Rather, it was intended to affirm that all people, including infants, are born under God's righteous condemnation, "Surely I was sinful at birth, sinful from the time my mother conceived me" (Psalm 51:5). Many people recoil at the very thought of this. From time to time people speak of the "innocence" of babies. However, the Bible is abundantly clear at this point, "Therefore, just as sin entered the world through one man, and death through sin, and in this way death came to all men, because all sinned" (Romans 5:12).

No one, not even infants are innocent. The sovereign election of God is our only basis of hope. If we believe infants go to heaven, on what ground do we make such a claim? Those who assume that babies are innocent and will go to heaven if they die before they reach the so-called "age of

[68] A. A. Hodge, *Westminster Confession of Faith* (1869; reprint ed., Carlisle, PA: Banner of Truth, 1958), chapter 10, section III.

accountability" are falsely claiming another way of salvation, namely, the way of innocence. This cannot be! There is only one way of salvation (John 14:6).

There are those that say babies are not saved but safe. However, this also presents us with the same problem. It assumes another way of salvation, namely, by "being safe." Anyone who ever goes to heaven, including infants, will do so not because they are innocent or safe but only because they have been saved.

The obvious deduction is, babies have no ability to believe the gospel. How then can they be saved? The *London Baptist Confession* gives the only consistent biblical answer,

> [They] are regenerated and saved by Christ through the Spirit, who worketh when, and where, and how he pleaseth. So also are all other elect persons, who are incapable of being outwardly called by the ministry of the Word [10.3].

They are saved because they are elect. The very fact that they die in infancy affirms their election. They are also redeemed. The blood that bought them is the same that covers all God's people. Christ died in their place. They are also regenerated by the Spirit even though they are incapable of being called by the ministry of the Word. But their salvation is just as sure as any of God's blood bought people.

Spurgeon states in his famous sermon entitled "Infant Salvation,"

> It has been wickedly, lyingly, and slanderously said of Calvinists, that we believe that some little children perish. Those who make the accusation know that their charge is false. I cannot even dare to hope, though I would wish to do so, that they ignorantly misrepresent us. They wickedly repeat what has been denied a thousand times, what they know is not true.... As for modern Calvinists, I know of no exception, but we all hope and believe that all persons dying in infancy are elect.... We have never taught the contrary, and when the charge is brought, I repudiate it and say, 'You may have said so, we never did, and you know we never did. If you dare to repeat the slander again, let the lie stand in scarlet on your very cheek if you be capable of a blush.' We have never dreamed of such a thing. With very few and rare exceptions, so rare that I never heard of them except from the lips of slanderers, we have never imagined that in-

fants dying as infants have perished, but we have believed that they enter into the paradise of God.[69]

In the same sermon, he draws several inferences from Scripture that support infant salvation, such as the goodness of the nature of God, the known character of our Lord Jesus Christ, the ways of grace, and the final unnumbered multitude of saved souls in heaven. While some might wish the Bible to be clearer on this subject, there is still sufficient reason to declare the issue settled.

(12) What is the best way to teach the doctrines of grace?

It has been facetiously said that those who come to embrace the doctrines of grace should immediately be locked up for about two years in order to learn how to balance zeal with wisdom. Many testify that it is like being reconverted. There is a new sense of joy and excitement. We want to tell everyone. Much grief will be avoided if the following guidelines are practiced by those who love these wonderful truths and want to share them:

1. *Love*—"Speaking the truth in love…" (Ephesians 4:15). A mean, forceful, argumentative spirit will do nothing but hinder the cause of truth.

2. *Gentleness and respect*—"Always be prepared to give an answer to everyone who asks you to give the reason for the hope that you have. But do this with gentleness and respect…" (1 Peter 3:15). The Lord will greatly use the person who has a winsome, gracious and humble disposition.

3. *Wisdom*—"A man has joy by the answer of his mouth. And a word spoken in due season, how good it is!" (Proverbs 15:23 NKJV). There is "a time to be silent and a time to speak" (Ecclesiastes 3:7). Some of us tend to be like "a bull in a china closet" when it comes to talking about these things. It is good that we begin with the milk of the Word and then go to the solid food (1 Corinthians 3:1–2), depending upon, of course, to whom we speak. Ask the Lord for a

[69] C. H. Spurgeon, *The Metropolitan Tabernacle Pulpit*, Vol. 7 (Texas: Pilgrim, 1978), 505-506.

wise sensitivity in knowing when and where to speak, what and how much to say.

4. *Expositorily*—Verse by verse, chapter by chapter, book by book, contextually accurate expository teaching and preaching will insure the declaration of the whole counsel of God (Acts 20:27). This kind of preaching will prevent dwelling unnecessarily on certain themes and topics. It will help us remember to use biblical language exclusively, not red-flag words and phrases, such as "Calvinism" or "irresistible grace" or "limited atonement." Such terms tend to put people on the defensive. They tend to hinder unbiased investigation and healthy dialogue. The doctrines of grace must be taught in their correct biblical context. When this is done we have the solid foundation of Scripture upon which to stand.

5. *Much study and thorough preparation*—"Do your best to present yourself to God as one approved, a workman who does not need to be ashamed and who correctly handles the Word of truth" (2 Timothy 2:15). More than a few well meaning Calvinists have ventured into territory they were not prepared to handle. We must be ready to give sound, well grounded, biblical answers. It is very unwise to blurt out statements we are not prepared to support from Scripture.

6. *Patience and careful instruction*—"Preach the Word... with great patience and careful instruction" (2 Timothy 4:2). Only God can write His truth upon our hearts. We must trust Him and not grow impatient with those whom the Lord has placed under our instruction. My own journey has been slow and many times I have been dull of mind and stubborn of heart. I still have such a long way to go. Most of us have to say the same. It is very important to remember this when teaching others.

7. *Prayerful dependence upon the Holy Spirit*—This is God's truth that we are proclaiming. He will make His Word effectual. We must saturate all our instruction in prayer. He will give us His strength to lovingly, wisely, gently, respectfully, humbly, knowledgeably, boldly, excitedly, patiently and faithfully make known His Word. If we do this, He will surely make fruitful our work for Him.

13. **What are some ways to promote loving, peaceful, healthy working relationships between those with differing views about Calvinism?**

(1) Strive to have a thorough understanding of Calvinism and related terminology—It is encouraging to see efforts like the 2007 Building Bridges conference, hosted by LifeWay and sponsored by Southeastern Baptist Theological Seminary and Founders Ministries. We need to promote more open and honest dialog about Calvinism and try to remove some of the misunderstandings of the past. I am convinced that most of the confusion and conflicts would cease if we would only lovingly strive for and insist on in-depth study and clarity of terms. Too often, we find it easier to attack caricatures and straw-dummies rather than listen to one another. A fitting response to those who ask you if you are a Calvinist is, "First share what you mean by the term and then I'll tell you if I am what you think." Caricatures and careless words create barriers. Encourage the use of biblical words as you aim for clarity and mutual understanding.

I deeply appreciate people like Dr. Daniel Akin, President of SEBTS who said, "Biblically-Illiterate SBC Pastors, NOT CALVINISM, is the Problem with the SBC! We're Talking about Calvinism... much of what I hear, today, is sloppy... it is ill-informed... theologically and biblically, we ought to be ashamed of ourselves!!! ... of some of the trite punch-lines that we hear coming out of the mouths of supposed leaders within the Southern Baptist Convention! Now lest you misunderstand me... I am not a five-point Calvinist... but I certainly believe when you critique something, you ought to do it with some semblance of knowing what you are talking about... but we don't do very good at it right now! Because we're not teaching the Bible... we're not teaching theology... and we, indeed, have lost sight of our calling...as the pastor/teacher of Ephesians 4:11... or if you like, the calling to be a pastor/theologian."[70] He goes out of his way to be fair and correct in what he says. May his tribe increase.

(2) Be teachable and willing to change wherever Scripture demands it, even if it's risky—Regretfully there are some who will not even consider the doctrines of grace. They have built walls of prejudice so high that conversa-

---

[70] Excerpt from sermon by Dr. Danny Akin (the South Carolina Baptist Convention's Pastor's Conference at Brushy Creek Baptist Church in Greenville, SC on Monday, November 13, 2006).

tion is almost impossible. A change in thier attitude seems as unlikely as leveling Mt. Everest. When Calvinism is mentioned, their words can be argumentative, imbalanced, heated and even hateful. Calvinism to them is so bad, wrong, heretical, unbiblical, divisive, controversial, non-Southern Baptist and just plain dumb that you dare not bring up the subject. There are even those whose retort goes something like this, "I don't care how much Scripture you show me to prove it, I still won't believe it!" Some don't believe the doctrines of grace for no other reason than that they simply do not want to. Others would just like to be rid of Calvinists. Despite passion and prejudice, we should always be willing to change any personal belief that conflicts with truth, no matter how long or how strongly we have held it, no matter how ingrained it has become, and no matter what we might have to lose if we change. Our resolve must be, in the words of Luther at the Diet of Worms, "I am captive to the Word of God."

(3) Love must characterize our thoughts, conversations and relation-ships—As debates and conversations take place across our convention, it is evident that we have often forgotten about love. Verse 2 of 1 Corinthians says, "And if I have (the gift of) prophecy, and know all mysteries and all knowledge; and if I have all faith, so as to remove mountains, but do not have love, I am nothing." Also John 13:34-35, "A new commandment I give to you, that you love one another; as I have loved you, that you also love one another. By this all will know that you are my disciples, if you have love for one another."

(4) Humility must prevail—It is sad to observe how some Calvinists can be puffed up even in light of such humbling doctrines. We Calvinists have done far more to hurt ourselves than we are willing to admit. There are not many things worse than an arrogant, over-zealous, mean spirited, know-it-all Calvinist.

I am likewise amazed at how non-Calvinists can react so angrily on the basis of tradition and hearsay regarding what should actually be called hyper-Calvinism. We must remember that God resists the proud but gives grace to the humble (James 4:6).

God forbid that any of us have a spirit of self-righteous pride about anything. One of my favorite verses is, "For who makes you differ from another? And what do you have that you did not receive? Now if you did indeed receive it, why do you boast as if you had not received it?" (1 Corinthians 4:7).

(5) Practice unity in diversity—This is one of the things that has made the SBC so great. There is room among us for differing views. Also, the gaps that separate us in the things about which we differ are not so wide. *The Baptist Faith and Message* is a huge umbrella under which we can walk. As Southern Baptists we all believe in the great Baptist distinctives: the authority and sufficiency of Scripture, the priesthood of the believer, salvation as God's gift of divine grace received through repentance and faith, regenerate church membership, the autonomy of the local church, the ordinances as symbols and reminders, baptism by immersion of believers only, absolute religious liberty for all, and the separation of church and state. We believe God is sovereign and that man is endowed with a will through which he makes authentic choices. All of us believe that every Christian is to have a passion and wholehearted commitment to fulfill the purposes of the church: worship, fellowship, discipleship, ministry, missions and evangelism.

I sincerely believe there is room for those who differ on election, predestination, free-will, foreknowledge, the extent of the atonement and the effectual call. Seldom is found two Baptists that agree on every fine point of theology. There are far more reasons to come together and embrace one another than to separate. Loving unity and healthy working relationships can be effectively maintained. I know this because I, for one, plus hundreds of other Southern Baptist Calvinists, are living proof. We work daily together with those who do not hold our theological position. Yet because we are brothers and sisters in Christ, and the building of the Kingdom of God is much bigger than our differences, we march together in love under the banner of the cross.

(6) Declare war on doctrinal ignorance—With some, words like "doctrine" and "theology" are, for all intents and purposes, irrelevant. Others would come close to calling them dirty words. Southern Baptists are notoriously ignorant when it comes to doctrine.

While we believe in unity in diversity, let us never relegate doctrine to a secondary place. Yes, there is great wisdom, for the sake of the Kingdom, in avoiding conflict and laying aside some of our differences in order to be unified. But let us never allow zeal for Kingdom growth to minimize doctrinal integrity. While some have spent too much energy in unnecessarily trying to prove a point, it is also true that not enough energy has been spent in soundly teaching our people. Doctrinal integrity must be of first importance.

We must encourage and promote doctrinal study whenever and wherever we can. First priority, of course, is the study of Scripture itself. Then there are almost unlimited resources in books, sermons, tapes, CDs and websites. It is quite interesting that many of the systematic theologies and books on Christian doctrine used prominently by our seminaries and colleges are Reformed, such as Wayne Grudem's *Systematic Theology* and Millard Erickson's *Introducing Christian Doctrine*. It is correct to assert that most of the best and greatest theological works in church history are written from the Reformed view.

One book that is easy to understand and helpful to place in the hands of those seeking a correct view of Calvinism is *Amazing Grace* by Timothy George, published by LifeWay. Dr. George is the President of Beeson School of Divinity in Birmingham. Instead of explaining the five points with the T-U-L-I-P, he uses the word R-O-S-E-S (R—radical depravity; O—overcoming grace; S—sovereign election; E—eternal life; S—singular redemption).[71]

(7) Prayer—Christian unity and our understanding of truth are matters that must be saturated in prayer. Christ prayed for the unity of His people (John 17:11, 21). It was one of the great desires of the Apostle Paul for all the churches (1 Corinthians 1:10; Ephesians 4:3,13). May God bring us together and produce loving unity throughout.

(8) Christ, first and foremost, must be our supreme love and passion— Dr. Akin said, "If the initials J.C. bring first to your mind the name of John Calvin rather than Jesus Christ and you fancy yourself more of an evangelist for Calvinism than Christ, then this latter word of concern is particularly for you. Never forget that the greatest theologian who ever lived was also the greatest missionary/evangelist whoever lived. His name is Paul."[72]

I am passionate about Calvinism because I sincerely believe it represents and espouses the great truths of Scripture that supremely honors God and exalts Christ more than any other system of theology. If the theology we embrace is not all about Christ and rooted in the whole counsel

[71] Timothy George, *Amazing Grace—God's Initiative—Our Response* (Nashville, TN: LifeWay, 2000), 60.
[72] Daniel Akin, "How Should Southern Baptists Respond to the Issue of Calvinism," *SBC Life* (April 2006), 10.

of God, we should abandon it. Forget any kind of theology that does not place Christ at the center. Spurgeon beautifully expresses my heart:

> "Again, the theme of a minister should be Christ Jesus in opposition to mere doctrine. Well, they are right in so doing, but I would not care myself to have as the characteristic of my preaching, doctrine only. I would rather have it said, "He dwelt much upon the person of Christ, and seemed best pleased when he began to tell about the atonement and the sacrifice. He was not ashamed of the doctrines, he was not afraid of threatening, but he seemed as if he preached the threatening with tears in his eyes, and the doctrine solemnly as God's own word; but when he preached of Jesus his tongue was loosed, and his heart was at liberty." Brethren, there are some men who preach the doctrine only, who are an injury, I believe, to God's church rather than a benefit. I know of men who have set themselves up as umpires over all spirits. They are the men. Wisdom will die with them. If they were once taken away the great standard of truth would be removed. We do not wonder that they hate the Pope, two of a trade never agree, for they are far more popish than he, they being themselves infallible. I am afraid that very much of the soundness of this age, is but a mere sound, and is not real; does not enter into the core of the heart, not affect the being. Brethren, we should rather preach Christ than election. We love election, we love predestination, we love the great doctrines of God's word, but we had rather preach Christ than preach these. We desire to put Christ over the head of the doctrine, we make the doctrine the throne for Christ to sit on, but we dare not put Christ at the bottom, and then press him down, and overload him with the doctrines of his own word."[73]

---

[73] C. H. Spurgeon, *The New Park Street Pulpit*, Vol. 3 (Grand Rapids, MI: Baker, 1994), 260.

15

It's Time to Blow the Trumpet

Joel the prophet called for the blowing of the trumpet in Zion in his day for the people to remember their rich spiritual heritage and return to their God (Joel 2:1,15). Today, it is time to blow the trumpet in our Southern Baptist Zion. It is time to call our people to remember our unique heritage.

It is time to blow the trumpet when many Southern Baptists don't even know what the doctrines of grace are and the term "Calvinism" is ridden with caricatures; when these life changing truths are considered more of a nuisance than anything else; when great biblical doctrines such as unconditional election and predestination are viewed as hindrances to evangelism, church growth and missions. Calvinists are certainly not opposed to church growth. We are, however, opposed to much of the current church growth movement and faulty evangelistic methods that defy sound, biblical principles.

It is time to blow the trumpet when the doctrines of grace are seen by many as divisive, unnecessary, confusing, too complex and inconsistent with the love and fairness of God; when college and seminary professors do not value these doctrines enough to give them fair and unbiased treatment in their classrooms; when fellow pastors and denominational workers label Calvinists as hyper-Calvinists. Many almost automatically equate the two. Usually people do not understand the difference. Hyper-Calvinism does not believe in the sincere universal offer of the gospel. It takes away from human responsibility. It tends to give little or no encouragement to the hungry and thirsty to seek the way of blessing—to go where the gospel water is flowing and bread is being offered.

It is time to blow the trumpet when Calvinists, after they are discovered tend to be pushed aside as not having a rightful place in current,

mainstream Southern Baptist life; when Calvinistic pastors are reluctant
to declare that God is God and that salvation is by grace alone for fear of
being dismissed from their pulpits; when many Southern Baptists are so
out of touch with Baptist history and biblical theology that they passively
neglect or even actively oppose these truths and those who preach them;
when churches won't seriously consider calling a pastor who believes these
"strange" things. The charge was once brought against me that I "practiced
Calvinism," as if I were practicing something horrible like witchcraft.

My wife and I attended the SBC in Atlanta in 1995. It was our ses-
quicentennial year as Southern Baptists. We enjoyed outstanding presentations and dramas about our history. Our founding fathers were honored.
As we sat there, we could not help but think of the irony we were witness-
ing. Here were thousands of Southern Baptists celebrating a wonderful
history and giving thanks for those who pioneered our great convention.
Yet if these outstanding spiritual giants of our past, such as Patrick Mell or
J.P. Boyce were to be present in contemporary Southern Baptist life they
would not be well received by many because of their strong and outspoken
Calvinistic beliefs.

In our denomination, the Calvinist more rightfully deserves the name
Southern Baptist than most, for both theological and historical reasons.
There are some "closet Calvinists" that are afraid to "come out." I am fully
cognizant of the risk involved. Ernest Reisinger, in his book entitled Reforming the Church writes the following timely statement,

> If men in every reformation were abused, misunderstood, misrepresent-
> ed, reviled, persecuted, ostracized, and excommunicated from organized
> religion, suffered mental and physical agony, and many times death, how
> can we expect to see reformation without cost (Luke 9 & 14)?
> What will it cost young pastors?
>
> (1) Denominational popularity and public approval. The work of reforma-
>   tion is not the way to climb the denominational ladder.
>
> (2) He will, at times, be in that awful task of tearing down some false super-
>   structure that has been built without a doctrinal foundation. This super-
>   structure was built by cheap, shallow, man-centered evangelism.
>
> (3) They may have to suffer at the hands of a large, unregenerate church
>   membership, and especially, from unregenerate and religiously ignorant
>   deacons and leaders.

(4) They may also have to suffer the pain of being misunderstood by the church leaders, fellow ministers, and more painful still, sometimes by their own loved ones (wives who do not understand their husband's position).

(5) Sacrifice financially, especially in some cases where carnal and ignorant church leaders will use money as a threat to drive preachers from the pulpit. But, along with these and other costs there comes the joy of a conscience void of offenses before God and man. What is that worth?[74]

What would a doctrinal reformation mean to Southern Baptists; one in which we returned to the solid biblical foundation of our founding fathers? The word R-E-F-O-R-M-A-T-I-O-N used as an acrostic will help answer this question,

R—*Reverential Fear of God*—Our desperate need is a renewal of the fear of God. Our day is characterized by Romans 3:18, "There is no fear of God before their eyes."

"The fear of the Lord is the beginning of knowledge" (Proverbs 1:7). Nothing will foster this kind of fear more than the recognition of the exalted, holy majesty of the most high God. To understand something of the perfect purity of the Almighty will produce genuine humility, true conviction of sin and Christlike holiness.

E—*Experiential Faith*—Predestination is God's eternal plan to conform us into the likeness of Jesus Christ (Romans 8:29). This is something we actually experience. It is a daily walk with God. It becomes the most exciting, refreshing, meaningful, exhilarating experience of our lives. Calvinism is a nickname for the gospel and the gospel teaches us that we can have a living vital relationship with the person of Jesus Christ. Cold indifference is replaced with warm hearted faith.

F—*Founders Faith Recovered*—The faith of the founders would once again thunder forth from our pulpits. Printed materials would be filled with unbiased treatment of the doctrines of grace. The great old confessions of faith would be honored, studied and used to help us become established in the faith. Missionaries would be sent to all parts of the world with this glorious gospel burning in their souls. College and seminary classrooms would echo the sound of reformed theology. How glorious it would be! I sincerely believe that day is coming.

---

[74] E. Reisinger, E., *Reforming the Church*, 12–13.

O—*Obedience to the Will and Purpose of God*—When we see God's bigness and His rule over all things, we see the absolute importance of complete dependence upon and explicit obedience to Him. To resist God's will is the most foolish, exhausting, futile, meaningless and wicked thing imaginable. Nothing else matters but Him and His purpose when our spiritual eyes are opened to see who He really is. It becomes the exclusive and only desire of our hearts to please our sovereign Lord.

R—*Reestablishment of Biblical Priorities.* I would never say that a return to the Reformed Faith would solve all our problems. However, it would provide a solid foundation. It would establish biblical parameters and principles that would keep our priorities in order. Our energies, talents, money and other resources would be channeled in the right direction. A weak or cracked foundation will always, sooner or later, cause a faulty superstructure. Misplaced priorities abound when correct doctrine is not held high.

M—*Motivation in Building the Kingdom of God*—Christ is Lord of lords and King of kings. His Kingdom is forever. When we become His children, we are then made Kingdom citizens. One day "the earth will be full of the knowledge of the Lord as waters cover the sea" (Isaiah 11:9). This is a guaranteed fact because God is sovereign. To maintain a positive, winning attitude is essential. Therefore we must live by Kingdom principles and conquer our world for Christ. He will not be defeated and His church will be triumphant. With renewed energy and holy enthusiasm we will obey the Great Commission. Evangelism and missions will take on new meaning.

A—*Acceptance of Calvinists in SBC Life*—What a blessed day it will be in our convention when those who hold to the faith of our founders are not looked upon with suspicion and disdainfully shunned! More than a few of our number have been needlessly threatened, criticized, misunderstood, and generally treated unfairly and hurt deeply.

T—*Truth*—"Then you will know the truth, and truth will set you free" (John 8:32). No price is too great to be permitted to live in the freedom of the truth. In Jesus' high priestly prayer He petitioned the Father, "Sanctify them by the truth; your word is truth" (John.17:17). The truth will do us nothing but good. Our task is to tell the truth, the whole truth and nothing but the truth, so help us God. The first question of the *Shorter Catechism* asks, "What is the chief end of man?" The answer, "Man's chief end is to glorify God, and to enjoy him for ever." Can anything bring more glory to Him than to uphold gospel truth?

I—*Immaturity Diminished*—It is the ministry of the gifted leaders of the church to equip the saints for the work of the ministry. The saints are to reach unity in the faith (Ephesians 4:13). Spiritual immaturity is rampant in our churches. Our people are not established in the faith. Doctrinal reformation will take giant strides in eliminating prolonged spiritual infancy.

O—*Omission of the Unnecessary*—There are many things that tend to corrupt the church. The temptation to drift into the Arminian error is ever present. Our admonition is to "be on your guard; stand firm in the faith" (1 Corinthians 16:13). Inadequate substitutes tend to take over when complete dependence is not placed in God. We tend to fall back on human wisdom and energy. We have been made stewards of the gospel. Every Christian generation has been given the awesome responsibility of preserving and maintaining God's truth. The doctrines of grace will help eliminate unnecessary things that tend to creep in.

N—*Necessary Worship, Adoration and Praise*—Nothing elicits more praise to God than to see Him in all His exalted splendor. Salvation belongs to our God. It is all of grace, from start to finish. All honor and glory belong to our blessed Christ. We are what we are only by His grace. His Name is to be forever praised. We must faithfully proclaim these truths, even amid opposition—in season and out (2 Timothy 4:1–5). The truth often divides (Matthew 10:34–39). When division occurs let's not automatically assume that it must not be of God. Truth must always be the basis of our unity. Preaching the truth will cause golden calves of tradition to fall, along with strongly held, unbiblical notions.

A few years ago I never would have dreamed of writing a book. However, in God's providence I have been placed in a set of circumstances in which God has shown me that I must share my journey in grace. As someone said to me, "If you are pushed hard enough and have enough passion about something, you can do more than you ever thought possible." There is nothing of which I am more sure, and about which I must speak than what I have written in this book.

Through my journey in grace, I have been encouraged and motivated by many outstanding heroes of the faith. Among them is the great reformer Martin Luther. He discovered, by divine revelation, that salvation is by grace through faith alone. His passionate desire was to help purge the church of its many forms of wickedness and heresy. With the fire of God's truth burning in his soul, he stood against the entire Catholic world of his day.

On October 31, 1517, at twelve o'clock, he nailed his Ninety-five Theses on the door of the castle church in Wittenberg, Germany, thus unwittingly launching the Protestant Reformation. It was the day before All Saints' Day because he knew people from all over the area would be visiting the church. What he wrote became something that no one, not even the pope could ignore. At the famous Diet of Worms (a special meeting in Worms, Germany), he was called upon to renounce his "heretical" faith. Surrounded by enormous opposition, he courageously gave the following statement that Dr. Roland Bainton records in his famous book about Luther, *Here I Stand*:

> Unless I am convicted by Scripture or plain reason—I do not accept the authority of popes or councils, for they have contradicted each other— my conscience is captive to the Word of God. I cannot and I will not recant anything, for to go against conscience is neither right nor safe. God help me. Here I stand, I cannot do otherwise.[75]

These words have given courage to thousands. Many times, especially when discouraged and tempted to give up, these words have inspired me.

While I would never be so presumptuous as to equate myself with Martin Luther, his courageous spirit puts fire in my bones. He was despised, threatened and excommunicated. Yet the gospel clearly sounded from his lips and pen.

Luther often expressed his faith in God by writing hymns. Of his thirty-seven hymns, his most famous was "A Mighty Fortress Is Our God." It was the victory anthem and battle cry of the Reformation. Based on Psalm 46, this song of courageous faith speaks of Luther's confidence in God as his refuge and strength. This great old hymn expresses my convictions as I continue my journey in grace:

A mighty fortress is our God,
A bulwark never failing;
Our helper He amid the flood
Of mortal ills prevailing.
For still our ancient foe
Doth seek to work us woe—

---

[75] R. H. Bainton, *Here I Stand: A Life of Martin Luther* (Nashville, TN: Abington Press, 1950), 144.

His craft and power are great,
And, armed with cruel hate,
On earth is not His equal.

Did we in our own strength confide,
Our striving would be losing,
Were not the right man on our side,
The man of God's own choosing.
Dost ask who that may be?
Christ Jesus, it is He—
Lord Sabaoth His name,
From age to age the same,
And He must win the battle.

Bibliography

A Faith to Confess: The Baptist Confession of Faith of 1689. Liverpool, England: Carey Publications, 1975.

Alleine, Joseph. *An Alarm to the Unconverted. London*: The Banner of Truth Trust, 1959.

Amazing Grace: The History and Theology of Calvinism. DVD. Draper, VA: The Apologetics Group, 2004.

Ascol, Thomas K., editor. *The Founders Journal*. Cape Coral, FL: Founders Ministries, 1990–2008.

_____. *From the Protestant Reformation to the Southern Baptist Convention: What Hath Geneva to Do with Nashville?* Cape Coral, FL: Founders Press, 1996.

_____, editor. *Reclaiming the Gospel and Reforming Churches: The Southern Baptist Founders Conference 1982–2002*. Cape Coral, FL: Founders Press, 2003.

Bainton, R. H. *Here I Stand: A Life of Martin Luther*. Nashville, TN: Abingdon Press, 1950.

Berkhof, Louis. *Systematic Theology*. Grand Rapids, MI: Wm. B. Eerdmans, 1939.

Boettner, Loraine. *The Reformed Doctrine of Predestination*. Phillipsburg, NJ: Presbyterian and Reformed, 1932.

_____. *The Reformed Faith*. Phillipsburg, NJ: Presbyterian and Reformed, 1983.

Boice, J. M. *Awakening to God*. Downers Grove, IL: InterVarsity, 1979.

Boyce, J. P. *Abstract of Systematic Theology*. Philadelphia: American Baptist Publication Society, 1887; reprint ed., Cape Coral, FL: Founders Press, 2006.

Broadus, John A. *Preparation and Delivery of Sermons*.1870, revised ed., NY: Hodder and Stoughton, 1898.

Carroll, B.H. *An Interpretation of the English Bible*. Nashville, TN: Broadman Press, 1942.

Carter, John F. *A Layman's Manual of Christian Doctrines*. Newton, MS: Published by Author, 1972.

Cheeseman, John, Philip Gardner, Michael Sadgrove and Tom Wright. *The Grace of God in the Gospel*. Carlisle, PA: The Banner of Truth, 1972.

Cole, Claude D. *The Bible Doctrine of Election*. Lexington, KY: Bryan Station Baptist Church, 1968.

Cole, L. D. *The Doctrines of Grace in the New Hampshire Confession of Faith*. Ottisville, MI: Baptist Book Trust, 1979.

Dagg, John L. *Manual of Theology*. Charleston, SC: Southern Baptist Publication Society, 1857; reprint ed., *Manual of Theology and Church Order*. Harrisonburg, VA: Gano Books, 1982.

Encyclopedia of Southern Baptists. 2 Vol. Nashville, TN: Broadman Press, 1958.

Erickson, Millard J. edited by L. Arnold Hustad, *Introducing Christian Doctrine*. Grand Rapids, MI: Baker Academic, 1992, 2001.

George, Timothy. *Amazing Grace—God's Initiative—Our Response*, Nashville, TN: LifeWay, 2000.

Gerstner, J. H. *A Primer on Free Will*. Phillipsburg, NJ: Presbyterian and Reformed, 1982.

Grudem, Wayne, *Systematic Theology*, Grand Rapids, MI: Zondervan, 1994.

Gunn, III, G. E. *The Doctrines of Grace*. Memphis, TN: Footstool, 1987.

Harrison, E. F., G. W. Bromiley and C. F. H. Henry, eds. *Baker's Dictionary of Theology*. Grand Rapids, MI: Baker, 1960.

Hobbs, H. H. *The Baptist Faith and Message*. Nashville, TN: LifeWay Christian Resources, 2000.

Hodge, A. A. *The Atonement*. Memphis, TN: Footstool, 1987.

_____. *Outlines of Theology*. 1879; reprint ed., Edinburgh: The Banner of Truth, 1983.

_____. *The Confession of Faith*. Carlisle, PA: Banner of Truth, 1869.

Hodge, Charles. *Systematic Theology*. Grand Rapids, MI: Eerdmans, 1979.

Kuiper, R. B. *For Whom Did Christ Die?* Grand Rapids, MI: Baker, 1959.

MacArthur, Jr., J. F. *Chosen for Eternity: A Study of Election*. Chicago, IL: Moody, 1989.

_____. *Ashamed of the Gospel*. Wheaton, IL: Crossway, 1993.

Manley, Sr., B., W. B. Johnson, R. B. C. Howell, R. Fuller and T. J. Nettles. *Southern Baptist Sermons on Sovereignty and Responsibility*. Harrisonburg, VA: Gano Books, 1984.

Martin, A. N. *The Practical Implications of Calvinism*. Carlisle, PA: The Banner Of Truth, 1979.

McLemore, R. A. *A History of Mississippi Baptists, 1780–1970*. Jackson, MS: Mississippi Baptist Convention Board, 1971.

Mell, P. H. *A Southern Baptist Looks at Predestination*. 1850; reprint ed., Cape Coral, FL: Christian Gospel Foundation, n.d.

_____. *Predestination and the Saints' Perseverance*. Charleston, SC: Southern Baptist Publication Society, 1851.

Murray, John. *Redemption Accomplished and Applied*. Grand Rapids, MI: Wm. B. Eerdmans, 1955.

Ness, Christopher. *An Antidote to Arminianism*. North Hollywood, CA: Puritan Heritage Publications, 1978.

Nettles, Thomas J. *A Foundation for the Future: The Southern Baptist Message and Mission*. Cape Coral, FL: Founders Press, 1997.

_____. *Baptists and the Doctrines of Grace*. DVD. Cape Coral, FL: Founders Ministries, 2004.

_____. *By His Grace and For His Glory*. Grand Rapids, MI: Baker, 1986; revised ed., Cape Coral, FL: Founders Press, 2006.

The New Convention Normal Manual for Sunday School Workers. Nashville, TN: Sunday School Board, Southern Baptist Convention, 1918.

New Encyclopedia Britanica.15th ed. Chicago, IL: Benton Publisher, 1980, S.V. "Baptists."

Owen, John. *The Death of Death*. Carlisle, PA: Banner of Truth, 1959.

Packer, J. I. *Evangelism & the Sovereignty of God*. Downers Grove, IL: InterVarsity, 1961.

_____. "Introductory Essay" in John Owen, *Death of Death in the Death of Christ*. Edinburgh: The Banner of Truth, 1967.

Palmer, E. H. *The Five Points of Calvinism*. Grand Rapids, MI: Baker, 1972.

Pink, A. W. *The Sovereignty of God*. Grand Rapids, MI: Baker, 1930.

Reisinger, Ernest C. and D. Matthew Allen. *Beyond Five Points*. Cape Coral, FL: Founders Press, 2002.

Reisinger, Ernest. C. and D. Matthew Allen. *A Queit Revolution: A Chronicle of the Beginnings of Reformation in the Southern Baptist Convention*. Cape Coral, FL: Founders Press, 2000.

Reisinger, Ernest. C. *A Southern Baptist Looks at the Biblical Doctrine of Election*. Cape Coral, FL: Founders Press, 2000.

_____. *Reforming a Local Church*. Pensacola, FL: Chapel Library, n.d.

_____. *Today's Evangelism*. Phillipsburg, NJ: Craig Press, 1982.

Reisinger, John G. *The Sovereignty of God in Providence.* Southbridge, MA: Crowne, 1989.

Rice, N. L. *God Sovereign and Man Free.* Philadelphia, PA: Presbyterian Board of Publication, 1850.

Seaton, W. J. *The Five Points of Calvinism.* Carlisle, PA: The Banner Of Truth, 1970.

Selph, R. B. *Southern Baptists and the Doctrine of Election.* Harrisonburg, VA: Sprinkle, 1988.

Sproul, R. C. *Chosen by God.* Chicago, IL: Tyndale, 1986.

Spurgeon, C. H. *A Defense of Calvinism.* Pensacola, FL: Chapel Library, n.d.

_____. *The Metropolitan Tabernacle Pulpit.* 63 Vols. Pasadena, TX: Pilgrim Publications, 1969–1980.

_____. *The New Park Street Pulpit.* 6 Vols. Pasadena, TX: Pilgrim Publications, 1981.

Steele, David N., Curtis C. Thomas. *The Five Points of Calvinism.* Phillipsburg, NJ: Presbyterian and Reformed, 1963.

Steele, David N., Curtis C. Thomas and S. Lance Quinn. *The Five Points of Calvinism.* 2nd ed. Phillipsburg, NJ: Presbyterian and Reformed, 2004.

Vincent, T. *The Shorter Catechism Explained from Scripture.* Carlisle, PA: Banner of Truth, 1980.

Taylor, Erma Leigh. *Co–operating Churches Under God.* Durant, OK: Published by Author, 1976.

To Whom He Will. Nundah, Queensland: Reformed Literature Information Society, n.d.

Waldron, S. E. *A Modern Exposition of the 1689 Baptist Confession of Faith.* Durham, England: Evangelical Press, 1989.

Waggoner, Brad J. and E. Ray Clendenen. *Calvinism: A Southern Baptist Dialogue.* Nashville, TN: B & H Academic, 2008.

Warburton, Ben A. *Calvinism*. Grand Rapids, MI: Wm. B. Eerdmans, 1955.

Williamson, G. I. *The Shorter Catechism*. 2 Vols. Phillipsburg, NJ: Presbyterian and Reformed, 1970.

_____. *The Westminster Confession of Faith for Study Classes*. Phillipsburg, NJ: Presbyterian and Reformed, 1964.

Zanchius, J., and A. M. Toplady. *The Doctrine of Absolute Predestination*. Grand Rapids, MI: Baker, 1977.

Printed in the United States
130211LV00002B/172-498/P

9 780978 571108